# A Student's Guide to MEXICAN AMERICAN Genealogy

Oryx American Family Tree Series

# A Student's Guide to MEXICAN AMERICAN Genealogy

By George R. Ryskamp
and Peggy Ryskamp

Oryx Press
1996

Printed and bound in the United States of America

∞ The paper used in this publication meets the minimum
requirements of American National Standard for Information
Science—Permanence of Paper for Printed Library Materials,
ANSI Z39.48, 1984.

Library of Congress Cataloging-in-Publication Data

Ryskamp, George R.
    A student's guide to Mexican American genealogy/by George R.
Ryskamp and Peggy Ryskamp.
        p.     cm.—(Oryx American family tree series)
    Includes bibliographical references and index.
    ISBN 0-89774-981-2
    1. Mexican Americans—Genealogy—Handbooks, manuals, etc.
2. Mexican Americans—Bibliography.   I. Ryskamp, Peggy.
II. Title.   III. Series: Oryx American family tree.
E184.M5R97   1996
929'.1'0896872073—dc20                                    96-19127
                                                              CIP
                                                               AC

# Contents

Researching your genealogy can lead you to exciting discoveries about the ways in which you are linked to your ancestors. Your musical talent, for example, could be directly tied to an ancestor who was a *mariachi*, a member of a Mexican strolling band.

# Chapter 1
# Why Do Mexican Americans Explore Family History?

Everybody enjoys the process of bringing parts together and creating something. Some people like working with crafts or sewing. They fit together pieces of wood or fabric in a particular way to make a finished product. Others enjoy the process of planning a party, combining the elements of a theme, invitations, games, and food. Still others like a good detective story, where the clues fit together to help determine "who done it." Even the simple process of putting together a puzzle gives a feeling of satisfaction.

Family history does the same thing. It brings together people, dates, places, and events and weaves them into a unique and exciting finished product. The best part is that the finished product is all about you. In the process of researching your Mexican American ancestry, you will make discoveries that can teach you more about yourself as well as your ancestors and your Mexican American heritage.

A person who is curious and likes to ask questions makes an excellent family historian. There is more to family history than simple names and dates. Before you begin researching your family lines, take time to think through some of the questions you would like to have answered about your unique Mexican American background, or in other words, all the pieces you would like to "fit together" to recreate your family history.

Do you wonder about the physical characteristics of your ancestors? Were they tall or short, heavy or thin? Perhaps you are particularly interested in how they dressed, or what they ate, or where they lived. The more questions you ask, the more you will realize how much there is that you would like to know. The process of answering these questions will allow you to piece together the distinctive history of your family.

## Understanding Yourself

As you make discoveries about your family members, you will find that you learn not only about them, but more about yourself. Have you ever had the opportunity to look at old family photographs? It may be hard to see in them anything similar to the people of today, until we remember that styles of dress and hair have changed over the years and that our custom of smiling for the camera was not always observed in other times and societies. This is where curiosity and good observation skills come into play. Take time to examine the faces in the pictures. Does the person have dark hair, or light? What is the shape of the face, the chin, the nose? Are the eyes wide-set or close together? Is the shape of the mouth and lips wide or thin? Once you begin to take note of these details, you may be surprised to find that you look more like your ancestors than you realized.

Of course, we inherit much more from our ancestors than our physical characteristics. The things that come easily for us, or that interest us, may also be genetically passed on. Perhaps you had ancestors who loved to sing, or dance, and these are things you enjoy as well. Or maybe you find that math is easy for you, and you have a relative who was also good with numbers. Remember that our ancestors may have possessed incredible talent in a field but never had the opportunity to use that skill fully because of their life's circumstances. For example, your grandfather may have been extremely gifted intellectually but was never able to attend school for more than a few years. Or an artistic relative may have expressed this talent in things made by hand—weaving at a loom, or making furniture—rather than by painting pictures on canvas. As you study the lives of your family

By talking with your family members, you can learn about fascinating aspects of your Mexican heritage like festivals or holidays. In this photo, Tarascan Indians of Michoacan, Mexico, travel to the burial lands of Janitzio Island to observe *El Día de los Muertos*, or Day of the Dead, in memory of their deceased kin.

members, look for ways in which they expressed themselves that may be similar to your own talents or hobbies. Perhaps you will discover a new hobby for yourself as you uncover evidence of an ancestor's skill in an artistic or practical endeavor.

## Understanding Your Ancestors

Of course, you are the only person who is just like you. Even if you have the same build as one of your relatives, or a similar nose, or identical coloring, you are the only person with your unique combination of personality, environment, and experiences. Remember that this is true for your ancestors as well. They lived in a different time, perhaps a time of political unrest or war. Many of them lived in different places than you do today, perhaps places with less economic opportunity. The combination of the time and place in which they lived, together with their individual personalities, shaped them into the people they became. Just as you want people to accept you for the person you are, we need to remember to do the same for our ancestors.

In a thought-provoking article in *American Heritage* magazine, the author asks, "Would you like your ancestors if you knew them?" Although the article focuses on life in frontier America, the same point could be made for life anywhere in the world as we go back 100 years or more. The lives people lived then were very different from ours. It helps to remember this as we learn about them. Try to understand the outside forces that may have been acting upon your ancestors before making judgements about the choices they made. Think about what you would have done in the same situation.

In many important ways our ancestors were just like us. They wanted to have enough to eat and to be warm during the winter. They wanted to be able to provide for their families and have fun once in a while. They wanted to be loved and accepted by family and friends. Perhaps the things that are the same about us, even going back many generations, are still more numerous than the things that are different.

## The Hispanic Surname System

The Hispanic surname system can be very helpful to you as you research your Mexican American family history. In searching your family lines, you will probably find that your ancestors have two surnames, or last names. This naming system is unique to Hispanic culture. It is used in Spain, Mexico, and all the countries of Central and South America, except Argentina and Brazil.

The Hispanic surname system gives you more information about your family history than other naming systems. Suppose that you find the birth certificate of your grandmother, and it gives her name as Maria Ximenez García. This tells you that her father's surname was Ximenez, and her mother's surname was García. Another way to say this is that her paternal surname was Ximenez, and her maternal surname was García. You can now add not just one but two names to your family tree, and you have more clues with which to continue your search. (See the pedigree chart on page 102 for an example of the Hispanic surname system.)

The Hispanic surname system differs significantly from that used in Anglo societies, that is, societies of people who are white and not of Hispanic descent. As you compare the two systems, the advantages provided to genealogists by the Hispanic surname system become clear. In the Anglo naming system, most women have traditionally dropped their maiden names once they have married, and have been known from then on by their husbands' last names. This can make it confusing to trace a woman's line of descent, since on many documents her maiden name is not listed. In Hispanic societies, however, the woman retains the surnames she was born with throughout her life, making it easier to find and identify her in documents.

As Mexican American culture has become a part of American culture, the Hispanic naming system has undergone changes. In some cases only the paternal surname has been retained. Or, you may find instances where an immigration official or government employee tried to fit Mexican immigrants' names into Anglo naming patterns and dropped the middle, or paternal, surname. However, with patience, imagination, and humor on the part of the family historian, these challenges can be overcome, and you will find that the double surname system can give you valuable clues for tracing your Mexican American ancestry. The surnames will serve as guideposts, pointing you in the right direction.

## Questions of Identity

What do you call yourself—Mexicano, Mexican American, or Chicana/Chicano? These terms are all used today to describe those people whose ancestors came from Mexico. Perhaps, however, you identify with a broader group, such as those whose ancestors came from elsewhere in Latin America or from Spain. In this case you might call yourself Latina/Latino, Hispanic, or Spanish American.

Whatever your choice, it is almost certain that your ancestors chose a different label. The term Chicano was defined by the prominent journalist Rubén Salazar in a 1970 column as "a Mexican American with a non-Anglo image of himself." If your parents or grandparents were active in the Chicano Rights Movements of the 1960s, they may have used only the term Chicana/Chicano, and considered the use of any other term to be reserved only for *tío tacos* (Uncle Toms) who were brainwashed by their Anglo neighbors to look down upon their Mexican heritage. A generation earlier your ancestors might have used only the term Mexican American, or, at least in New Mexico, Spanish American.

*Tejano, nuevomexicano,* and *californio* are other terms you might have heard in regard to Mexican American identity. *Tejano* refers to Mexican settlers in Texas. *Nuevomexicano* refers to Spanish-speaking settlers of New Mexico. And *californio* refers to Mexican settlers in California. These terms are still used by some people today to describe Mexican Americans in Texas, New Mexico, and California.

Today, many scholars and political activists agree that taking pride in your Mexican heritage is more important than what you choose to be called. Be respectful of others' preferences for one term over another. If you feel that someone is using a term you find offensive, explain to them why you feel that way and suggest an alternative. Do not assume that they are trying to offend you; they may simply be misinformed.

## Adoption and Nontraditional Families

Many people of all ethnicities are adopted or live in nontraditional family situations—with a single parent, grandparent, or other relative, for example.

If you are adopted or live in a nontraditional family situation, you may be wondering whether you will be able to trace your roots. The good news is that you can research your family history no matter what your family situation. You may face more challenges, but meeting them will make your final results all the more satisfying.

Adoption records are sealed until the adoptee is eighteen years old. This is designed to protect both biological parents and adoptive parents who may have reasons for not wanting a child to find his or her biological parents. After the age of eighteen, if you decide to have your adoption records unsealed, you can also sign up on an adoption register. Adoption registers match biological parents with adopted children. Of course, for this to work, both parties must sign up on the register.

However, you do not need to find your biological parents in order to conduct genealogical research. Your adoptive parents may have some basic information about your birth parents. If you bring up your interest in researching your genealogy in a sensitive and honest manner, your parents may be responsive and willing to provide you with whatever information they have.

Another option is to research the genealogy of your adoptive family. After all, you are a member of their family now. They will probably be thrilled at your interest in their ancestors and eager to share information with you. This can be a way to become even more closely connected to the family that adopted you.

If you live with a single parent or in another kind of

nontraditional family, you may still be able to research the genealogy of one family line. This is in itself a great accomplishment. In fact, professional genealogists recommend researching only one family line at a time. If the parent you do not live with is Mexican American, and that side of your family tree interests you, talk to the parent you live with about how to proceed. You may be in touch with relatives from one side of your family even if you are not in touch with your parent. These relatives may be able to help you in your research. Again, sensitivity, honesty, and patience will go a long way in getting people to help you in your search.

## Finding Spanish-Language Books

You will notice that some of the materials listed in the **Resources** sections of this book are in Spanish. Some are published by Spanish-language publishers in the United States, while others are published in Mexico or Spain. Consult with your librarian on how to track down Spanish-language books. Your chances of finding them in your local library are better if you live in a large city, in California or the Southwest, or in another area with a large Spanish-speaking population. Even if the books are not owned by your library, you may be able to order them through interlibrary loan.

If your librarian is unable to acquire a book for you but you know the name of the publisher and the city where it is located, you can contact the publisher directly by looking up its address and phone number in the *International Literary Market Place* (New Providence, NJ: R. R. Bowker, 1996), a reference book that lists publishers around the world. Look for the *ILMP* in your library's reference section. If your city has a Spanish-language bookstore, check to see if they have the book there, or ask if the bookstore may be able to order the book for you from a distributor.

Finally, if you have access to a computer, a modem, and the Internet, type in a search using keywords such as "Spanish books" or "Mexican books." A number of Spanish-language publishers, book distributors, and bookstores have home pages from which you can search for and sometimes even order materials. Check, for example, the home page of the Spanish Book Distributor at http://www.netpoint.net./sbd/sbd.html; the home page of the Spanish-Speaking Bookstore at http://centerstage.net/chicago.literature/bookstores/Spanish-Speaking.html; and the Publishers' Catalogs Home Page at http://www.light.com/publisher/index.html.

Of course, if you are lucky enough to be able to travel to Mexico, plan to visit a library there to find the books listed in this volume as well as many others.

# Resources

## STARTING YOUR EXPLORATION

**Ashabrenner, Brent.** *The Vanishing Border: A Photographic Journal Along Our Border with Mexico.* **New York: Putnam, 1987.**

This photo-essay uses interviews, commentary, and history to provide a portrait of life along both sides of the border between the United States and Mexico.

**Augenbraum, Harold, and Stavans, Ilan, eds.** *Growing Up Latino: Memoirs and Stories.* **New York: Houghton-Mifflin, 1993.**

Twenty-five eloquent Latino voices shed light on the Hispanic experience. Sandra Cisneros and Richard Rodríguez are among the featured writers.

**Carlson, Lori M.** *Cool Salsa: Bilingual Poems on Growing Up Hispanic in the United States.* **New York: Henry Holt, 1995.**

Themes of Hispanic American teenage life, such as difficulty learning English, ethnic prejudice, and questions of identity, are explored by writers such as Oscar Hijuelos and Sandra Cisneros.

**Hoobler, Dorothy, and Hoobler, Thomas.** *The Mexican American Family Album.* **New York: Oxford University Press, 1994.**

Excerpts from journals, letters, oral histories, and newspaper articles are accompanied by photographs, drawings, and maps to form a portrait of the Mexican American culture and community.

**Lankford, Mary D.** *Quinceañera: A Latina's Journey to Womanhood.* **Brookfield, CT: Millbrook Press, 1995.**

A Mexican American girl undergoes a coming-of-age ritual in an example of the preservation of a rich Mexican American culture in American communities. The quinceañera celebration, which occurs when a girl is fifteen years old, is derived from an Aztec ceremony.

**Martinez, Elizabeth Coonrod.** *Sor Juana: A Trailblazing Thinker.* **Brookfield, CT: Millbrook Press, 1995.**

A readable biography for young people. The true story of a seventeenth-century Mexican girl who was forbidden a formal education and faced opposition from the Spanish Inquisition, yet went on to become one of history's greatest Mexican writers and thinkers.

**Sinnott, Susan.** *Extraordinary Hispanic Americans.* **New York: Children's Press, 1991.**

This collection of biographies is arranged in chronological order to give you a sense of the many accomplishments of Hispanic Americans throughout history, from the 1400s to the present.

**Stein, R. Conrad.** *The Mexican Revolution 1910–1920.* **New York: New Discovery Books, 1995.**

A handy, accessible reference on one of the most important events in Mexican history. Includes descriptions of battles and profiles of leading figures such as Pancho Villa and Emiliano Zapata.

**Wolf, Bernard.** *Beneath the Stone: A Mexican Zapotec Tale.* **New York: Orchard Books, 1995.**

Illustrated with stunning photographs, this text provides a glimpse into a culture that, while ancient, is still vibrant today. Readers follow the story of Leo Ruiz, a young boy who wants to follow in his father's footsteps and become a weaver.

# BEGINNING YOUR FAMILY HISTORY SEARCH

**Platt, Lyman D. "Hispanic-American Records and Research." In *Ethnic Genealogy: A Research Guide*. Edited by Jessie Carney Smith. Westport, CT: Greenwood Press, 1983.**

This article describes Mexican American research using case studies. It will give you a sense for what awaits you in your family history search.

**Ryskamp, George R. *Tracing Your Hispanic Heritage*. Riverside, CA: Hispanic Family History Research, 1984.**

Chapter 1 discusses the meaning of Hispanic family history research and reasons for undertaking it.

**Villaseñor, Victor. *Rain of Gold*. Houston: Arte Público Press, 1991.**

Several generations of the author's family history are incorporated into this novel. It may help to inspire you as you see what can ultimately be accomplished.

# HISPANIC NAMES

**Arce, Rose Marie, and Junco, Maité. *Bebes Preciosos: 5001 Hispanic Baby Names*. New York: Avon, 1995.**

Although intended for parents-to-be, this book will be fascinating for anyone interested in the origins and meanings of Hispanic names.

**Platt, Lyman D. *Hispanic Surnames and Family History*. Baltimore: Genealogical Publishing Co., 1996.**

Platt spent twenty-five years preparing this book, the first comprehensive work analyzing Hispanic surnames and the most extensive bibliography of Hispanic family histories ever published. The book discusses thousands of Hispanic surnames in the United States and Latin America. Find out information about your surname and discover whether one of the family histories mentioned in this book might be about your family.

**Santos, Richard G. *Origin of Spanish Names: Como Te Llamas Y Porque Te Llamas Así*. San Antonio: Richard G. Santos, 1981.**

This book explores the origins of Spanish names and surnames. Spanish names are one of the legacies of Spanish rule in Mexico.

## SOURCES OF INFORMATION FOR ADOPTEES

**Adopted and Searching/Adoptee-Birthparent Reunion Registry**
**401 East 74th Street**
**New York, NY 10021**
**212-988-0110**

**Adoptees and Birthparents in Search**
**P.O. Box 5551**
**West Columbia, SC 29171**
**803-796-4508**

**Askin, Jayne, with Molly Davis. *Search: A Handbook for Adoptees and Birthparents*, 2d ed. Phoenix: Oryx Press, 1992.**

A comprehensive guide to registers and searching aids.

**The International Soundex Reunion Registry**
**P.O. Box 2312**
**Carson City, NV 89702**
**702-882-7755**

# Chapter 2
# Your Mexican American Heritage

As you stand in the Plaza de Tres Culturas in the heart of downtown Mexico City, you can see evidence of the three cultures of Mexico. In front of you lie the ruins of the magnificent primary temple of the Aztec; to your left, the elegant colonial-era cathedral; and behind you, the Zócalo, the central square flanked by the residence of the Mexican president and other governmental office buildings. These sights represent the three cultures that make up Mexico: Indian, Spanish, and the new culture that arose from the blending of those two: Mexican. As a Mexican American, your family's traditions and way of life in the United States add a fourth culture to these three. For some of you, these Mexican American traditions may only be a generation or two old, while for many families in New Mexico, southern Colorado, and south Texas, the traditions stretch back twelve generations or more.

You can take great pride in the Indian part of your heritage. The Aztec people built incredible cities. Other peoples like the Tlaxcalan, who fought with Hernán Cortés against the Aztec, were equally impressive in their accomplishments, as were earlier indigenous cultures in central Mexico. The Aztec themselves referred to Teotihuacan, the marvelous city of one of these cultures, as "the city of the gods," finding it hard to believe that mortal men could build such a place.

As you stand on top of the Pyramid of the Sun at Teotihuacan, in southeastern Mexico, the massive pyramids and buried ruins that remain of this civilization attest to its grandeur and leave even seasoned travelers overwhelmed by its size and magnificence. At the height of its power, the city covered a geographical area larger than Imperial Rome. But

The Indian heritage of Mexico is a colorful and important part of Mexican culture. Above, a boy participates in an Indian dance group in Mexico.

with less than half the population of Imperial Rome, the Indian inhabitants of Teotihuacan enjoyed a much higher standard of living than their contemporaneous Roman counterparts. The Mayan culture of southeastern Mexico, the Zapotec of Veracruz, and the Toltec and Olmec of central Mexico all enjoyed similar periods of greatness.

Your Indian heritage, however, is not limited only to great ruins. Popular Mexican celebrations, such as the Day of the Dead, were first celebrated by Indians. A rich variety of foods, words, place names, and cultural characteristics have been transferred from Indian culture to Mexican culture and, in turn, to other cultures throughout the world. For example, foods such as corn tortillas, tamales, mole sauce, tomatoes, and chilies, as well as the Mexican penchant for bright colors, are all legacies of this Indian heritage. Other Mexican traditions such as mural painting and the use of certain herbs for healing are also gifts passed on for many generations by Indian peoples and their descendants.

## *Mestizo* Society

In Mexico one often hears the word *mestizo*, meaning a mixture of Spanish and Indian. Up to 80 percent of the Mexican population is *mestizo*, according to government census figures. In genetic heritage and cultural heritage, you likewise are a *mestizo* who can take great pride in the accomplishments of both the Indian and the Spanish cultures.

Benito Juárez, a full-blooded Zapotec Indian from Oaxaca, overcame incredible odds to become an educated and successful lawyer. He became independent Mexico's first effective leader in 1861, when he was elected president.

In many ways you could use the term *mestizo* to refer to Mexico itself. In fact, there are those who say that Mexico was born from the union of the conquistador Hernán Cortés and La Malinche, the Aztec woman who was his guide and lover. Starting with the conquest of the Aztec by Cortés in 1519–1521, the history of Mexico brims with periods of conflict and cooperation, often simultaneous, between Spanish and Indian cultures and peoples.

## Spanish Contributions to Mexico

During the years following the Mexican Revolution of 1910 to 1928, scholars as well as popular speakers and politicians emphasized the great contributions made to Mexico by Indian cultures, while negating the historical reality of the major contributions made by Spanish culture. Perhaps the single greatest Spanish cultural contribution to Mexico was the Catholic religion, which is today thoroughly a part of the Mexican culture. Unlike the Anglo-American culture, which adopted a policy of driving North American Indians out of their lands and onto reservations that were often thousands of miles from their homelands, the Spanish adopted a policy consisting primarily of assimilation and merger, in large part as a result of the strong influence of the Spanish Catholic Church. Although many Indians converted voluntarily to Catholicism, many were also no doubt swayed by the fact that people who practiced other faiths often faced execution by the Spanish.

The Spanish were hardly benevolent rulers. They enslaved, killed, and stole from the indigenous peoples of Mexico. They brought with them diseases, such as smallpox, to which the Indians had no immunity. For the Spaniards, Indians were a source of cheap labor for their gold and silver mines in Mexico. While the Spanish settlers grew rich, the Indians grew poorer, and many were displaced from their native lands. The colonial era lasted for 300 years, leaving a legacy of displacement, poverty, illiteracy, and racial prejudice.

In addition to the Catholic religion, the Spaniards brought with them the full breadth of their culture. This includes the richness of the Spanish language, which has given voice to geniuses such as the Spanish writer Miguel de Cervantes, author of *Don Quixote*, and modern Mexican philosophers and writers such as Octavio Paz. The first universities in the Americas, the first printing presses, the first operas, and the first theaters were all established in Mexico by the Spanish, in most cases more than a century before anything comparable existed in the Anglo-American colonies of North America. In fact, a visitor to colonial Philadelphia or New York and Mexico City would have found Mexico City to resemble an elegant and beautiful European city, with the North American cities resembling country towns in comparison.

The peninsula separating the Gulf of California from the Pacific Ocean is called Baja California. It was first explored by the Spaniards in the 1530s, but attempts to colonize the region were unsuccessful. It is now a state of Mexico. Alta California was the term used by the Spanish to refer to their possessions north of Baja California. Today, the term Alta California is used to refer to the northern part of the peninsula.

Your Mexican American heritage has a long history in the area that is now the United States. The first two cities founded in the United States, Saint Augustine, Florida (1565), and Albuquerque, New Mexico (1598), were both settled by the Spanish. By 1800, through conquest, colonization, and diplomacy, the Spanish Empire in what is now the United States extended from Florida on the east coast to California on the west coast and ran as far north as what is today Seattle, Washington.

During the next half century, from 1803 to 1852, the Spanish areas of the United States were transferred through sale, treaty, or war from Spain to Mexico, and ultimately to the United States. Territory that was once held by Mexico that is now part of the United States has come to be called Aztlan, named after the original Aztec homeland. These areas were inhabited by Native Americans before they were settled by Mexicans. The Mexican settlers clashed with Anglo cowboys and cattle barons who sought to expand the American West. Aztlan became a symbol of the struggle of Mexican Americans for civil rights in the 1960s.

## A Conflict Between Mexico and the United States: The History of Texas

The history of Texas is a fascinating, often bloody saga of the tensions and dramas between the United States and Mexico. When Mexico declared independence from Spain in 1821, American residents were allowed to enter directly into Texas, which was then still a part of Mexico. By 1830 the number of English-speaking immigrants in Texas outnumbered the Spanish-speaking Mexican population.

In 1835 war broke out between the Anglo settlers (Texans) and the Mexican government. Some *tejanos* (Texans of Mexican ancestry), who were greatly outnumbered by Anglo settlers, joined in the fight against Mexico for Texan independence. Most, however, remained loyal to Mexico, unsure of what they would gain from independence.

The Texans overwhelmed Mexican military units in surprise attacks and managed to drive out the majority of Mexican troops from Texas. The city of San Antonio was captured by the Texans, and a provisional government was set up.

Antonio López de Santa Anna, the Mexican president and military commander, mobilized a large army to crush the

Texan rebellion. The famous defense of the Alamo, a Franciscan mission in San Antonio, ensued in February, 1836. Texans and pro-independence *tejanos* defended the mission from Santa Anna's forces. Many Mexican soldiers died during the siege. All of the Texan and *tejano* defenders of the Alamo were killed. Soon after the fall of the Alamo, hundreds of Texans were massacred in the town of Goliad at the behest of Santa Anna.

On March 2, 1836, a few days before the siege of the Alamo ended, Texas declared its independence from Mexico. Sam Houston was named commander-in-chief of the Texan armies. In the battle of San Jacinto on April 21, 1836, Houston led a surprise attack and defeated the larger Mexican army. Santa Anna was captured and forced to recognize the independence of Texas. In 1836, Houston was elected president of the Republic of Texas. Although most Texans sought annexation to the United States, the Republic of Texas was not allowed admission into the Union because of its acceptance of slaveholding. In 1845, Texas was annexed by the United States, becoming the twenty-eighth state of the Union. The loss of Texas was a great blow to Mexico. After Texas achieved independence, many *tejanos* felt like strangers in their own land as Anglos' anti-Mexican feelings hardened.

## Establishing the Border

Texas was not the only land that would be taken from Mexico. In 1846, motivated primarily by the doctrine of Manifest Destiny (the concept that the United States should ultimately rule from coast to coast), the United States invaded Mexico under the leadership of General Zachary Taylor. The battles of this war took the Americans all the way to Mexico City, which was captured in 1847. Santa Anna signed the Treaty of Guadalupe Hidalgo in 1848. Under the terms of this treaty, the Rio Grande became the border between Texas and Mexico. Soon after, it was discovered that there was extensive mineral wealth in what is now southern Arizona. The United States persuaded Mexico

Mexican immigrant laborers were among the diverse groups of workers who helped build railroad lines across the United States. These workers, natives of Jalisco, Mexico, worked in Maryland for the Pennsylvania Railroad.

to sell the region, using the argument that the proposed Southern Pacific Railroad connecting newly acquired California with the rest of the country should be built through Arizona. In an 1852 arrangement called the Gadsen Purchase, the southern parts of Arizona and New Mexico, including the city of Tucson, Arizona, were purchased from the Mexican government for $15 million. This established the current boundary between the United States and Mexico.

With these transfers of lands that had been part of Mexico, more than 100,000 people of Mexican and Spanish descent from the western borders of Louisiana to the California coast became new citizens of the United States. It is possible that your ancestors were among them. The most heavily populated area acquired from Mexico was New Mexico, with a population of about 60,000 people. In California, Arizona, and Texas, the English-speaking Anglo-American population very quickly outnumbered the Mexicans.

## Twentieth-Century Mexican Emigration

Many of you have no ancestors who were in the United States before 1848. Since that period there has been a continual flow of Mexican immigrants into the United States. The greatest numbers have come between 1910 and 1925 and from 1945 to the present. It is not surprising that the greatest numbers have emigrated during times of prosperity and expansion in the United States and economic or political instability in Mexico. This is particularly true for the period from 1910 to 1925, when many Mexicans fled north to escape the devastating Mexican Revolution. In fact, more than 10 percent of the Mexican population left Mexico during the years following the revolution. That revolution marked the end of thirty-four years of rule by President Porfirio Díaz and his supporters.

During the *Porfiriato*, as the rule of Díaz was called, Mexico had made great progress in organizing its financial and political institutions. As was also the case in the United States at that time, however, this progress had not been accompanied by a recognition of the needs of the working classes. In the United States these issues were confronted by a series of progressive governments such as that of President Theodore Roosevelt. In Mexico there were no such progressive governments, and the working class, including many Indians, were never given the means to reap the benefits of economic development. Díaz's regime was notorious for its corruption and its intolerance of political dissent. Political opponents were ruthlessly persecuted. The result of these social and political conditions was the Revolution of 1910 to 1928. The Mexican Revolution was led by a landowner named Francisco I. Madero, who won the presidency in 1911. But the revolution raged on as various groups fought for power. Most of the revolutionaries sought economic and social reforms. (In some ways, however, the process of achieving a fair distribution of wealth was never completed. The uprisings in the early 1990s were in protest of the same problems.)

Mexican immigrants fleeing the violence and poverty caused by the revolution came to work in the agricultural fields and factories of the Southwest. *Colonias* were communities formed by Mexican immigrant farmworkers near the agricultural areas where they worked. *Colonias* quickly grew crowded as increasing numbers of Mexican immigrants came to work in the fields of the Southwest and California. *Barrios* were Mexican American communities in urban areas. They were often in poor, run-down neighborhoods, but they provided a cultural center for new and established Mexican immigrants. Mexican shops, restaurants, and theaters helped Mexican Americans to adjust to life in the United States and to preserve aspects of their heritage. The largest *barrio* was in Los Angeles. San Antonio and El Paso also had large *barrios*.

Mexican Americans often established mutual aid societies, called *mutualistas*, in *colonias* and *barrios* to help new immigrants cope with the difficult adjustment process. In addition to organizing social and cultural events, *mutualistas* provided assistance to immigrants in need of help.

Many Mexican Americans dedicated their energies to the U.S. cause in World War I. Mexican Americans were the largest U.S. ethnic group to fight in that war, and many Latino soldiers were decorated with medals and honors.

During the 1930s and 1940s, while the United States struggled through the Great Depression and World War II, very few Mexicans immigrated. Many Mexican Americans served in the U.S. armed forces in World War II (as they had in every war since the Civil War). They served valiantly, often with a very high casualty rate. Many earned distinguished military decorations, including the Congressional Medal of Honor. Mexican Americans and Anglo-Americans came to know and appreciate each other as they fought in military units together. You may have a parent, grandparent, or uncle who served in the United States armed forces. The stories they tell will illuminate your understanding of the struggles and triumphs of Mexican Americans in the first half of the twentieth century.

## The Zoot Suit Period

As a result of the immigration wave following the Mexican Revolution, a new generation of Mexican American teenagers came of age in the United States in the 1940s. Adolescence is always a difficult time, but for these teens it was especially painful because they had to grapple with discrimination and racism as well.

Particularly in El Paso and Los Angeles, Mexican American teenage boys became known as *"pachucos." Pachucos* developed a distinctive style of dress. This style of dress was known as the "zoot suit." The zoot suit consisted of a long coat, baggy pants that fit tightly at the ankles, and a hat with a broad brim that sometimes bore a feather. Mexican American teenage girls, known as *"pachucas"* or *"cholas,"* also had a unique style of dress. They wore short, tight black skirts, black sweaters, and fishnet stockings.

Like all teenagers, Mexican American teens sought freedom and individuality. Many had been taught in school to be scornful of their Mexican heritage, so they tried to distance themselves from their families and sought support from neighborhood friends. Conflicts sometimes erupted between neighborhood groups as they fought over favorite meeting places. Competition for these hangout spots was fierce because many other facilities, such as roller-skating rinks and movie theaters, were restricted or forbidden to the Mexican American teens.

*Pachucos* became a focus of American anger and anxiety during World War II. As Mexican American neighborhoods grew in Los Angeles, the city became increasingly racially segregated. Mexican Americans were often restricted from using theaters, restaurants, and public facilities such as parks and swimming pools. Many schools were segregated, and students could be punished for speaking Spanish. Mexican

In the 1940s, many Mexican American youths proclaimed their identity with a new style of dress. The broad-shouldered coats and baggy pants with tight ankles that many youths wore were known as zoot suits.

Americans faced discrimination in employment and housing.

The widening gap between the Anglo and Mexican American communities in Los Angeles was worsened by misguided Anglo fears of Mexican American teenage "gangs" running wild and committing crime and violence. The news media began to focus on the *pachucos*, suggesting to some that the problem was out of control. A special grand jury was convened in Los Angeles to investigate the Mexican American "problem."

Incidents of violence against Mexican Americans were common. Several cases of blatant injustice on the part of the criminal justice system occurred. The greatest tragedy, however, was the *Pachuco* Riots in 1943. The violence began after a group of sailors, who claimed to have been attacked by a group of Mexican American youths, took justice into their own hands. Sailors and other members of the armed forces rioted in the streets of Los Angeles, assaulting anyone wearing a zoot suit. They beat their victims with impunity; indeed, following the beatings, the police often arrested not the assailants but their Mexican American victims.

Two days after the riots had begun, the press began to publish reports that the *pachucos* planned to strike back. Thousands of Anglo-Americans took to the streets to preempt the attack they believed was about to occur and continued on the sailors' trail of violence. The Mexican American community fought back, and the Navy shore patrol finally stepped in to stop the riots after four days of violence. But instead of criticizing the unprovoked violence, the news media seemed to support the attacks against Mexican Americans.

## The Postwar Era

Conditions for Mexican Americans in Los Angeles and elsewhere gradually improved in the years after the *Pachuco* Riots. When Mexican American veterans returned from World War II, they were unwilling to live as second-class citizens in the country for which they had risked their lives. Seventeen Mexican Americans received Congressional Med-

Mexicans have historically emigrated in the largest numbers during times of U.S. prosperity or Mexican economic or political instability. Many became farmworkers in border states, like these laborers in El Paso, Texas, who sought to benefit from the American economic upswing following World War II.

als of Honor for bravery in World War II. Government loans for all veterans made it possible for Mexican Americans to purchase property. Slowly, segregation in schools and residential areas came to an end in California and other parts of the Southwest. Organizations such as the Mexican American Political Association, the Latino Issues Forum, and the American G.I. Forum were formed during the late 1940s. Mexican Americans organized to make certain that their voices were heard and to end discrimination.

Following World War II, as economic conditions in the United States improved dramatically, Mexican immigrants again flocked across the border. The new immigrants often worked in menial jobs as farm laborers or domestic help. In the 1960s, 1970s, and beyond, the descendants of Mexicans who had immigrated to the United States in the nineteenth century and first half of the twentieth century were moving into a wide variety of professions and activities. Today Mexican Americans are found in all professions and walks of life. Many have contributed their talents to the fascinating study of their heritage. More than 1,500 scholars from all academic disciplines are members of the National Association of Chicano Studies.

## Progress Despite Discrimination

This progress has required active participation and effort on the part of many Mexican Americans. Discrimination against Mexican Americans throughout the southwestern United States and in the cities of the North, where many migrated to work in factories, was rampant. Despite the long history of Mexican Americans in the United States, they were often treated as second-class citizens. At a Chicago movie theater in the 1920s, Mexican Americans were required to sit in the balcony instead of the main-floor seats. The administration of President Herbert Hoover announced a plan in 1931 to deport Mexicans who had immigrated to the United States illegally, but even legal immigrants who had lost their immigration documents were sometimes deported.

Because of the hard work of many individual Mexican Americans, the Chicano Civil Rights Movement, a movement to fight for Mexican American rights, gained strength in the 1960s and 1970s. It has made great strides in gaining for Mexican Americans an equal position in American society. Its activities have ranged from organizing farmworkers, led by César Chávez and the United Farm Workers (UFW), to student movements for better education. Many organized groups such as *La Raza Unida*, LULAC (League of United Latin American Citizens), and the American G.I. Forum contributed to the fight for equal rights. Latino lawyer associations exist in large cities throughout the United States, as well as in many smaller cities in the Southwest.

Successful Mexican American businesspeople are found in both large and small companies across the nation. Mexican

César Chávez, the son of immigrant farmworkers, devoted his life to the Mexican American farmworkers. In 1962, Chávez founded what would later be called the United Farm Workers (UFW), a labor union that fights for the social and economic rights of agricultural laborers.

American performing artists and movie stars, including Carlos Santana and Anthony Quinn, have helped shape the nature of American popular music and cinema. Outstanding writers such as Richard Rodríguez have explored the difficult and rewarding bicultural landscape trod by many Mexican Americans as well as masterfully addressing issues that resonate with Americans of every ethnicity. Mexican Americans such as the journalist Rubén Salazar, the playwright Luis Valdéz, the scholar Octavio I. Romano, the publisher José Armas, politicians Gloria Molina and Henry Cisneros, and writers, artists, dancers, and athletes too numerous to mention have enriched American society beyond measure.

Today, while there is still much to be done in the United States in the battle against discrimination, Mexican Americans are active in all walks of life, from the arts to business to politics, and are making significant contributions to their communities.

## Migrant Workers

At the beginning of the twentieth century, the American Southwest was thriving economically. The agricultural sector began to develop, and many Mexican Americans and Mexican immigrants took jobs as farmworkers. Because different crops were ready to be harvested in different seasons, the farmworkers moved from place to place to pick whichever crops were in season there. They traveled between New Mexico, Colorado, California, Arizona, and Texas, picking crops of cotton, fruit, and vegetables.

Women and children often worked in the fields, too. Entire families put in long days for low wages and lived in spartan quarters. When no crops were in season, men found work on construction crews or doing other physical labor. Women took jobs as domestic workers for Anglos.

Growers had no trouble finding willing workers, especially with the large numbers of Mexicans who immigrated after the Mexican Revolution. But this situation made it nearly impossible for migrant workers to achieve higher wages and better working conditions. Because they were paid so little, workers could not afford to go on strike. They were aware that their actions would have little effect anyway, since they could be easily replaced.

Things became especially difficult for migrant farmworkers during the Great Depression, which began in 1929. Anglos whose livelihoods had been ruined by the drought that struck Arkansas, Oklahoma, and Texas came to California to find work. They were often hired instead of workers of Mexican origin. Anti-Mexican sentiment grew as Mexican workers were seen as an economic threat.

Despite the difficulties of organizing for their rights, Mexican workers did have some success in forming unions. The Confederación de Uniones Obreras Mexicanas (The Confederation of Mexican Workers) and La Union de Trabajadores del Valle Imperial (The Union of Workers of the Imperial Valley) organized Mexican farmworkers during the 1920s and had some success in achieving their demands.

When the United States labor pool was drastically reduced during World War II, Mexican workers were brought in by the *bracero* program to work for American farmers. Life for the *braceros* was difficult. They came without their families and moved from farm to farm, working for thirty cents an hour and living in poor conditions.

Today, immigrants from Mexico and other Latin American countries continue to perform the backbreaking labor that brings fresh fruits and vegetables to American salad bars and dinner tables. Thanks to the work of dedicated activists like César Chávez, many of these workers now belong to unions that help to protect their rights.

## Mexican American Women

Mexican American women have historically contributed in important ways to the success of the Mexican American community. This has been particularly evident in the immigrant struggle in the United States. As the *barrios* grew and Mexican American businesses began to open, more Mexican American women were employed in retail and clerical jobs. During World War I, when many Mexican American men went off to battle, Mexican American women worked in garment factories, fish canneries, and food-processing plants to supplement family income.

One woman in particular stood up for the rights of Mexican and Mexican American migrant farmworkers in the 1960s. Her name is Dolores Huerta. Huerta was born in 1930, the child of migrant workers. Her mother eventually saved enough money to open her own hotel, where she rented rooms to poor farmworkers. When they could not afford the rent, she often allowed them to stay free of charge. Young Dolores inherited her mother's generous spirit, industriousness, and commitment to justice. After spending several years as a schoolteacher, Huerta decided to join the Community Service Organization (cso), a Latino civil rights organization. In 1962 she joined forces with fellow cso member César Chávez to found the National Farm Workers' Association. The name was later changed to the United Farm Workers Union. The organization grew rapidly and gained political clout. One of its most noteworthy accomplishments was the organization of the Delano Grape Strike in 1965, which eventually resulted in gains for formerly exploited grape pickers in California. Huerta continues her work to this day.

In the 1970s many Mexican American women participated in the feminist movement, forming organizations such as the Chicana Service Action Center, which provided job training to Latinas, and the Los Angeles–based Comisión Femenil Mexicana Nacional, which encouraged Latinas to assume positions of leadership. During this decade, Vilma Martínez became the president of the Mexican American Legal Defense and Education Fund. Mexican American women continued to rise to positions of political power in the 1980s and 1990s, as well as making great strides in the arts, sciences, business, and other fields.

Mexican American writer Sandra Cisneros, who has published novels, short stories, and poems which have received numerous literary awards, is one of the most gifted voices in American literature today. Estela Portillo-Trambley is an

Mexican American women have historically been important contributors to the struggle for equal rights for Mexican Americans. This young woman was part of a group who marched on the California capitol building in Sacramento in 1971 to protest discrimination against Americans of Mexican descent.

award-winning poet, playwright, and author. In the art world, Mexican American mural painter Judith Boca helped pioneer the Mexican American mural movement in Los Angeles. Painter Barbara Carrasco creates powerful works that challenge traditional views of Mexican American women. The American music scene would not be what it is today without the contributions of Mexican American musicians such as Linda Ronstadt, Joan Baez, and Selena. Long the principal dancer of the San Francisco Ballet, Evelyn Cisneros has been consistently recognized for her contributions to the arts.

Other notable Mexican American women include Katherine Ortega, a businesswoman and the second Latina to serve as U.S. Treasurer. Gloria Molina was the first Latina elected to the California State Legislature, the Los Angeles City Council, and the Los Angeles County Board of Supervisors. Ana Navarette is a key organizer in the Service Employees International Union's movement "Justice for Janitors" and as such has worked to secure decent labor conditions among Latinos.

Mexican American women have made especially great progress in the last twenty-five years. Chicanas are found in all professions and businesses, although in some cases they must still exert extra effort to overcome the prevalent "machismo" (strong emphasis on masculine pride) of Mexican American society and the sometimes lingering discrimination of mainstream American society. For information about some of the many successful entrepreneurial Chicanas, visit your local library and ask for recent issues of the magazine *Hispanic Business*.

## Mexico's Jewish Heritage

While conducting your genealogical research, you may be surprised to learn that you are of Jewish descent even if your family is Catholic. This is because many of the Jews who immigrated to Mexico in the past were compelled to convert to Christianity in the country they came from. Others con-

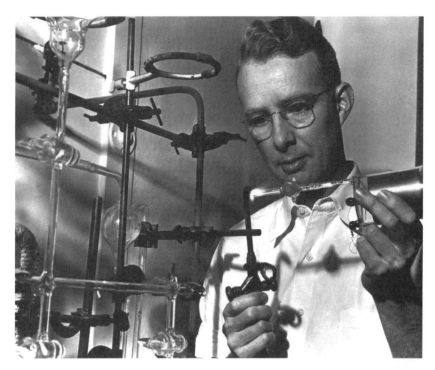

To be a Mexican American is to be part of a proud and distinguished history in the United States. Included in the long list of notable Mexican Americans is Luis Alvarez, the University of California professor of physics who won the Nobel Prize in 1968 for his work in radio-activity.

verted voluntarily in Mexico in the process of becoming acculturated to Mexican society.

In 1391, the Jews who had settled in Spain began to be forcibly converted to Christianity. The Spanish Inquisition was established in 1478 at the behest of Ferdinand II and Isabella I to detect and punish converted Jews and Muslims who continued to practice their religious beliefs secretly. The Spanish Inquisition dealt extremely harshly with Jews suspected of religious infidelity. Many were tortured until a confession of heresy was obtained; those who refused to recant were burned at the stake as part of the notorious ceremony known as *auto-da-fé*. At the height of its power, the Inquisition was instituted in all of Spain's colonies.

Amazingly, the Spanish Inquisition was not formally abolished until 1834.

The persecution of the Jews culminated in their formal expulsion from Spain in 1492. Jews subsequently spread throughout the Mediterranean basin; in Europe, North Africa, and the Middle East. Shortly after Christopher Columbus discovered the New World in 1492, Sephardic Jews—the branch of European Jews who lived in the Iberian Peninsula during the Middle Ages along with their descendants—began to immigrate to the islands of the Caribbean and Latin America.

The Sephardic settlers brought many aspects of Spanish-Judeo culture to the Americas, including the language known as Judezmo or Ladino, which combines elements of medieval Castilian with Hebrew and other languages. However, many of the *conversos* (converts from Judaism to Christianity) who either fled or were expelled from Spain during the Inquisition continued to conceal their Jewish identity in Mexico because the Spanish monarchs had issued a decree banning Jews from all of Spain's dominions. In fact, the most active foreign tribunal of the Spanish Inquisition was established in Mexico City.

Some Jews opted to migrate once again in search of a safe haven, while others chose to remain in Mexico. Many of the descendants of these Jewish settlers in Mexico can be found in what is today the American Southwest, in such states as New Mexico, Texas, and Arizona. While some members of the Jewish community in Mexico openly practice their religious faith, others have steered clear of any public expression of their religious identity. These "crypto-Jews" use Christianity as a veneer for their Jewish faith to avoid prejudice and persecution. As a result, many Mexicans and Mexican Americans are unaware of their Jewish heritage because they were raised in ostensibly Catholic homes.

Another group of Jews settled in Mexico in the 1920s and 1930s. These young immigrants were sent to Mexico by their parents to protect them from the pogroms (organized massacres), poverty, and political instability raging in Eastern Europe at that time. Many of these Jewish immigrants to Mexico became peddlers on the streets of Mexico City. As their fortunes improved, many opened their own businesses, joined synagogues, and carried on Jewish traditions.

## A Rich Tradition

Even as you participate in the broader stream of American society, don't lose sight of the wealth of Mexican American culture that is available to you. Mexican American art, music, and literature (in Spanish and in English) reflect and contribute to that culture. So do traditional holidays and festivals such as *Cinco de Mayo* (Fifth of May) and *El Día de la Virgen de Guadalupe* (The Day of the Virgin of Guadalupe). Your Mexican American heritage also includes traditions unique to your family. Perhaps your Christmas includes such traditions as *tamales*, a family *posada*, or *luminarias* lining the front sidewalk. If you enjoy these traditions, you might plan to pass them on to your children.

As you begin the search for your ancestors, look for their participation in the great and small moments of Mexican American history. Were they among the *tejanos* at the Alamo? Did they help found San Diego in 1769, or Los Angeles in 1781? Were they among the many Mexican Americans from Texas and California who fought in the Civil War? Did they come to the United States during the Mexican Revolution, riding the tops of packed railroad cars? Perhaps they were political refugees who helped fight the oppressive government of Porfirio Díaz by writing or working against it from the American side of the border. Perhaps they were among the migrant farmworkers who, in the 1960s and 1970s, fought for social justice under the leadership of César Chávez. Or they may be among the New Mexicans who have maintained a unique Hispanic culture in the only state where Spanish shares with English the status of an official language. Wherever you find them, you will see that your ancestors contributed in small or great ways to the rich cultural heritage that is yours today as a Mexican American.

# Resources

## MEXICAN AND MEXICAN AMERICAN HISTORY

**Abalos, David T.** *The Latino Family and the Politics of Transformation.* **Westport, CT: Praeger Publishers, 1993.**

More than a social or historical study, this book looks at the personal politics of a changing contemporary Latino family in the United States.

**Alessio Robles, Vito.** *Francisco de Urdiñola y El Norte de la Nueva España.* **Mexico City: Editorial Porrua, 1981.**

Francisco de Urdiñola was a sixteenth-century colonizer and Spanish governor of northern New Spain. This book tells about his life, as well as events during this time period. (Text in Spanish.)

**Alford, Harold J.** *The Proud Peoples: The Heritage and Culture of Spanish-Speaking Peoples in the United States.* **New York: New American Library, 1972.**

This book offers an in-depth and celebratory look at the culture and history of Hispanics in the United States.

**Almaraz, Felix D., Jr.** *The San Antonio Missions and Their System of Land Tenure.* **Austin: University of Texas Press, 1989.**

The San Antonio missions played an important role in the Spanish settlement of Texas. Land records used in compiling this book are rich with potential family history value for the Hispanic American researcher.

**Arno Press Collection.** *The Chicano Heritage.* **New York: Arno Press, 1976.**

This collection of fifty-five titles deals with Chicano subjects and includes bibliographies, original studies, and archive guides. Titles include *Aspects of the Mexican American Experience* and *The Bracero Program in California.*

**Ashford, Gerald.** *Spanish Texas, Yesterday and Today.* **Austin: Jenkins Publishing Co., 1971.**

If you have ancestry from Texas, this book can give you details of the history during the time period in which your ancestors lived.

**Bannon, John F.** *Spanish Borderlands Frontier, 1513–1821.* **Albuquerque: University of New Mexico Press, 1974.**

An excellent and readable history of Spanish exploration and settlement in the United States.

**Beerman, Eric.** *España y la Independencia de los Estados Unidos.* **Madrid: Editorial MAPFRE S.A., 1992.**

Spain and Spanish citizens played key roles in the fight for independence in the United States, as described in this book. (Text in Spanish.)

**Beezley, William H.; French, William E.; and Martin, Cheryl E., eds.** *Rituals of Rule, Rituals of Resistance: Public Celebrations and Popular Culture in Mexico.* **Wilmington, DE: Scholarly Resources Inc., 1994.**

Essays explore the use of public holidays and celebrations both for controlling the masses, especially the Indians, and as a means of resistance by them to the dominant Spanish culture. For advanced readers.

**———, and Ewell, Judith, eds.** *The Human Tradition in Latin America: The Nineteenth Century.* **Wilmington, DE: Scholarly Resources Inc., 1989.**

Through biographical essays about a wide range of individuals in Latin American history, both famous and unknown, we are given a better understanding of the history and people of Latin America.

————, and MacLachlan, Colin M. *El Gran Pueblo: A History of Greater Mexico.* Englewood Cliffs, NJ: Prentice-Hall, Inc., 1994.

A well-documented history of Mexico, including the immigrant cultural extension into the United States.

Brinckerhoff, Sidney B., and Faulk, Odie B. *Lancers for the King: A Study of the Frontier Military System of Northern New Spain with a Translation of the Royal Regulations of 1772.* Phoenix: Arizona Historical Foundation, 1965.

This pivotal study analyzes the Bourbon military system on the northern New Spain frontier at the end of the eighteenth century. A source for advanced readers interested in military history.

Brookman, Philip, and Gómez-Peña, Guillermo, eds. *Made in Aztlan.* Los Angeles: Centro Cultural de la Raza, 1986.

Aztlan is the mythical home of the Aztec, which some believe was in the area now occupied by the United States. The Centro Cultural de la Raza in Los Angeles sponsors Chicano, Mexican, and Indian cultural and political activities.

Campa, Arthur. *Hispanic Culture in the Southwest.* Norman: University of Oklahoma Press, 1993.

The author discusses and analyzes the traditional folklore of Hispanic society in New Mexico and elsewhere in the Southwest.

————. *Treasure of the Sangre de Cristos, Tales and Traditions of the Spanish Southwest.* Norman: University of Oklahoma Press, 1994.

Oral tradition and folklore are important aspects of Mexican American culture. This book explores the stories that have shaped Hispanic culture.

**Casteñeda, Carlos E.** *Our Catholic Heritage in Texas, 1519–1936, Vols. I–V.* **Austin: Von Boeckmann-Jones Co., 1936–58.**

These volumes comprise a definitive study of the Catholic Church in Texas. Most Mexicans and Mexican Americans follow the Catholic faith.

**Chipman, Donald E.** *Spanish Texas, 1519–1821.* **Austin: University of Texas Press, 1992.**

Did any of your ancestors live in Texas? If so, check this history of the Spanish colonial period of Texas for an understanding of political events during the time that they lived.

**Cruz, Gilbert R.** *Let There Be Towns: Spanish Municipal Origins in the American Southwest, 1610–1810.* **College Station: Texas A & M University Press, 1988.**

The urban societies created by the Spanish colonizers as they created towns in the American Southwest are the focus of this study. If your ancestors were Spanish settlers in the Southwest, see this volume.

**De Leon, Arnoldo.** *The Tejano Community, 1836–1900.* **Albuquerque: University of New Mexico Press, 1992.**

If your ancestors lived in Texas, you will want to read this history of Mexican Americans in Texas from the time of independence up to the beginning of the twentieth century.

**De Varona, Frank.** *Bernardo de Galvez.* **Austin: Steck-Vaughn Co., 1991.**

This is the biography of a great Hispanic hero of the American Revolution.

————. *Hispanic Presence in the United States: Historical Beginnings.* Miami: Mnemosyne Publishing Company, 1993.

> Written by a Hispanic scholar, this volume provides an excellent introduction to the history of Hispanics in the United States.

**Deutsch, Sarah.** *No Separate Refuge: Culture, Class and Gender on an Anglo-Hispanic Frontier in the American Southwest, 1880–1940.* New York: Oxford University Press, 1987.

> A frontier is by definition a place where two countries or cultures meet, and thus is often the site of tensions and conflicts. This book explains those tensions and conflicts as they related to culture, class, and gender in the American Southwest. For advanced readers.

**Dobyns, Henry F.** *Spanish Colonial Tucson: A Demographic History.* Tucson: University of Arizona Press, 1976.

> If you have ancestry from Tucson, this meticulous analysis of the population of that city during the colonial period may be of interest to you.

**Fernández-Shaw, Carlos M.** *The Hispanic Presence in North America from 1492 to Today.* New York: Facts on File, 1991.

> State by state, this book explores the Hispanic impact in the United States in areas ranging from names to culture.

**Gann, L. H., and Duignan, Peter J.** *The Hispanics in the United States: A History.* Boulder, CO: Westview Press, 1986.

> This book represents a unique viewpoint on Hispanics in the United States.

**Gutiérrez, Ramón A.** *When Jesus Came the Corn Mothers Went Away: Marriage, Sexuality, and Power* *in New Mexico, 1500–1846.* Stanford, CA: Stanford University Press, 1993.

> The conflict between Indian and Hispanic cultures and their merger are explored and explained through the analysis of marriage, sex, and family patterns in New Mexico up to the American occupation. For advanced readers with an interest in anthropology and history.

Jackson, Jack. *Los Mesteños: Spanish Ranching in Texas, 1721–1821.* College Station: Texas A & M University Press, 1985.

> Much of the cowboy culture of the American West has its origin in the Spanish ranches of Texas. This book explores the historical antecedents of that culture. Of particular interest are the excellent illustrations.

Jones, Oakah L., Jr. *Los Paisanos: Spanish Settlers on the Northern Frontier of New Spain.* Norman: University of Oklahoma Press, 1979.

> A noted scholar of the Spanish borderlands looks at the lives and roles played out by the common folk who made up the bulk of the settlers in northern New Spain.

Kiser, George C., and Kiser, Martha W. *Mexican Workers in the United States: Historical and Political Perspectives.* Albuquerque: University of New Mexico Press, 1979.

> A series of essays on the history of Mexican immigration to the United States, the *braceros* (legal agricultural workers), repatriation of illegal workers, and border industrialization programs. It includes policy statements from U.S. and Mexican presidents and other officials, U.S. and Mexican newspaper editorials and articles, and personal testimonials. These personal accounts may be of particular interest; consider comparing them to the memories of your own relatives.

**LaFarelle, Lorenzo G.** *Bernardo de Galvez: Hero of the American Revolution.* **Austin: Eakin Press, 1992.**

The contribution to the American cause of this Spanish general and governor of Louisiana was equal to that of the French Lafayette, but he has gone essentially unnoticed in American history books.

**LeVine, Sarah.** *Dolor y Alegría: Women and Social Change in Urban Mexico.* **Madison: University of Wisconsin Press, 1993.**

Through a series of interviews with Mexican women, the author explores the changes that have taken place in Mexican society during the last fifty years.

**Liebman, Seymour B.** *The Inquisitors and the Jews in the New World: Summaries of Procesos, 1500–1810, and Bibliographical Guide.* **Miami: University of Miami Press, 1974.**

————. *The Jews in New Spain.* **Miami: University of Miami Press, 1970.**

As Hispanics, especially in New Mexico, have recently become aware of their Jewish roots, the study of the Spanish Inquisition's persecution of Jews described in these books has taken on greater significance for the Mexican American family historian.

**Martínez, Oscar J., ed.** *The U.S.-Mexico Borderlands: Historical Contemporary Perspectives.* **Tucson: University of Arizona Press, 1995.**

The editor has brought together both scholarly essays and primary documents to illuminate key issues in borderlands studies. His emphasis on conflict and interdependence presents a background to anyone seeking to better understand the historical perspectives of the relationship between the United States and Mexico. For advanced readers.

**Matovina, Timothy M.** *The Alamo Remembered: Tejano Accounts and Perspectives.* **Tucson: University of Arizona Press, 1995.**

This collection of firsthand reports and memoirs shows that some of the residents of San Antonio of Mexican origin found their greatest allegiance not with Santa Anna, but with their fellow San Antonians who were Anglo-Americans.

**Mayo, Samuel H.** *A History of Mexico: From Pre-Columbia to the Present.* **Englewood Cliffs, NJ: Prentice-Hall, Inc., 1978.**

This is a good one-volume history of Mexico.

**McWilliams, Carey.** *North from Mexico: The Spanish-Speaking People of the United States.* **Westport, CT: Praeger Publishers, 1990.**

First published in 1949, and updated by Matt S. Meier to cover the period 1945 through 1988, this classic text explores all aspects of the Chicano experience in the United States—including family, employment, education, assimilation, and political, cultural, and economic issues.

**Menchaca, Martha.** *The Mexican Outsiders: A Community History of Marginalization and Discrimination in California.* **Austin: University of Texas Press, 1995.**

This study, covering the Spanish colonial period to the present day, delves deeply into interethnic relations in Santa Paula, California, to document how the residential, social, and school segregation of Mexican Americans became institutionalized in a representative California town.

**Miller, Hubert J.** *José De Escandón: Colonizer of Nuevo Santander.* **Edinburg, TX: New Santander Press, 1980.**

This biography tells the story of the colonizer of the Rio Grande Valley, covering south Texas and Tamaulipas, Mexico.

**Moore, James Talmadge.** *Through Fire and Flood: The Catholic Church in Frontier Texas, 1836–1900.* **College Station: Texas A & M University Press, 1994.**

This excellent volume traces the development of the Catholic Church in Texas during the nineteenth century.

**Moorhead, Max L.** *The Presidio: Bastion of the Spanish Borderlands.* **Norman: University of Oklahoma Press, 1975.**

A classic study of the line of forts created by the Spanish in the southwestern United States and northern Mexico to defend the northern borders of Spanish civilization.

**Navarro, Armando.** *Mexican American Youth Organization: Avant-Garde of the Chicano Movement in Texas.* **Austin: University of Texas Press, 1995.**

A comprehensive assessment of this extremely vocal and visible part of the 1960s Chicano protest movement.

**Nevins, Albert J.** *Our American Catholic Heritage.* **Huntington, IN: Our Sunday Visitor, Inc., 1972.**

This well-illustrated one-volume history of the Catholic Church in the United States recognizes the Hispanic contribution to Catholicism in this country.

**Nostrand, Richard L.** *The Hispano Homeland.* **Norman: University of Oklahoma Press, 1992.**

In this excellent social and demographic history of Hispanic culture in southern Colorado and New Mexico, the author uses sources that are also useful to genealogists.

**Officer, James E.** *Hispanic Arizona, 1536–1856.* **Tucson: Arizona Historical Society, 1989.**

An excellent one-volume study of the Hispanic presence in Arizona for nearly 300 years before Anglo Americans came.

**Pitt, Leonard.** *The Decline of the Californios: A Social History of the Spanish-Speaking Californians, 1846–1890.* **Berkeley: University of California Press, 1966.**

This social history traces the decline of the Spanish-speaking population in California from a position of social and political dominance to that of a discriminated minority during the last half of the nineteenth century.

**Rausch, Jane M., and Weber, David J.** *Where Cultures Meet: Frontiers in Latin American History.* **Wilmington, DE: Scholarly Resources, Inc., 1994.**

This collection of essays explores the concept of the frontier in Latin American history. It is often viewed negatively as a place where civilization has failed, as compared with the view of the frontier in the United States as the place where our national character was forged.

**Roberts, Susan A., and Roberts, Calvin A.** *New Mexico.* **Albuquerque: University of New Mexico Press, 1991.**

If your ancestors are from New Mexico, you will enjoy this excellent one-volume history of "the land of enchantment."

**Roca, Paul M.** *Paths of the Padres Through Sonora: An Illustrated History and Guide to Its Spanish Churches.* **Tucson: Arizona Pioneers' Historical Society, 1967.**

Emphasizing the key role of the Catholic Church in the northern expansion, this book offers well-illustrated evidence of the extent of the early mission effort in Sonora, Mexico, and southern Arizona.

**Ruiz, Ramón Eduardo.** *Triumphs and Tragedy: A History of the Mexican People.* **New York: W. W. Norton and Co., 1992.**

The author suggests that every aspect of Mexican history is additional evidence of the exploitation and destruction of Indian culture by the dominant Spaniards. This bias is both the strength and the weakness of this history of Mexico. Unfortunately, the lack of footnotes makes it impossible to check the author's sources for some of his more controversial positions.

**Sánchez, George J.** *Becoming Mexican American: Ethnicity, Culture and Identity in Chicano Los Angeles, 1900–1945.* **New York: Oxford University Press, 1993.**

Utilizing 2,500 naturalization records of Mexican Americans who applied to become citizens of the United States in the early part of the twentieth century, as well as other local sources, the author traces the development of a growing identity among Mexican Americans in Los Angeles.

**Sánchez, Joseph P.** *Spanish Bluecoats: The Catalonian Volunteers in Northwestern New Spain, 1767–1810.* **Albuquerque: University of New Mexico Press, 1990.**

The exciting story of a regiment of volunteers from Catalonia and eastern Spain who served as military escorts for Spanish colonization efforts on the western coast from San Diego, California, to Seattle, Washington. The footnotes reveal the author's use of a wide variety of historical sources from which a family historian could derive an excellent family history.

**Saragoza, Alex M.** *Fresno's Hispanic Heritage.* **Fresno, CA: San Diego Federal Savings and Loan Association, 1980.**

This book tells a fascinating story about Hispanic culture and contributions to the community.

**Sedillo López, Antoinette, ed.** *Historical Themes and Identity: Mestizaje and Labels.* **New York: Garland Publishing, 1995.**

Racial mixture and the identity labels that accompany it played an important role in the development of Mexico and its people. This book explores in a series of essays the conflicts and compromises inherent in the process of *mestizaje,* or mixing of races or cultures.

**Seed, Patricia.** *To Love, Honor, and Obey in Colonial Mexico.* **Stanford: Stanford University Press, 1988.**

Utilizing court records dealing with marriage conflict cases from the Archdiocese of Mexico, this author explores the Mexican institution of marriage and the social concepts of honor, love, and obedience that supported and surrounded it.

**Simmons, Marc.** *The Last Conquistador: Juan De Oñate and the Settling of the Far Southwest.* **Norman: University of Oklahoma Press, 1991.**

A biography of the founder of New Mexico, and the story of the challenges faced by the original settlers of the state.

**Stagg, Albert.** *The Almadas and Alamos, 1783–1867.* **Tucson: University of Arizona Press, 1978.**

This history of one of the most important families of the city of Alamos in northern Mexico makes excellent use of the wide variety of local history resources available in Mexico.

**Tijerina, Andres.** *Tejanos and Texas Under the Mexican Flag, 1821–1836.* **College Station: Texas A & M University Press, 1994.**

The role of Mexican Texans in the years before the Texas war for independence is analyzed in this work by a noted Texan historian.

Torre, Adela de la, and Pesquera, Beatriz M. *Building with Our Hands: New Directions in Chicana Studies.* Berkeley: University of California Press, 1993.

This collection of essays illustrates the experiences and struggles of Mexican American women from the colonial Spanish period to the modern era.

Vásquez, Nadine M. *Sinaloa Roots: An Account of the 1781 Expedition to Alta California and Ancestral Records of Early California Settlers, 1723–1808.* Carmichael, CA: Nadine M. Vásquez, 1974.

This account of the 1781 expedition to Alta California (the northern part of the Baja peninsula) includes the family history of its settlers.

Weber, David J. *Foreigners in Their Native Land: Historical Roots of the Mexican American.* Albuquerque: University of New Mexico Press, 1973.

————. *The Mexican Frontier, 1821–1846, The American Southwest Under Mexico.* Albuquerque: University of New Mexico Press, 1982.

————. *Myth and History of the Spanish Southwest.* Albuquerque: University of New Mexico Press, 1988.

————. *The Spanish Frontier in North America.* New Haven, CT: Yale University Press, 1992.

Since their appearance only a few years ago, these works have become the definitive works on the Spanish borderlands and the historical roots of the Mexican American population.

Yeager, Gertrude M. *Confronting Change, Challenging Tradition: Women in Latin American History.* Wilmington, DE: Scholarly Resources, Inc., 1994.

A fascinating collection of readings on the role of women

in Latin American history, with emphasis not only on their activities in political and economic spheres, but on their domestic role as well.

## MEXICAN AMERICAN CULTURE

**Blea, Irene Isabel.** *La Chicana and the Intersection of Race, Class, and Gender.* **Westport, CT: Praeger Publishers, 1991.**

The roles and stereotypes of women in Mexican American society are explored and analyzed.

**Deck, Allen Figueroa, and Dolan, Jay P., eds.** *Hispanic Catholic Culture in the U.S.: Issues and Concerns.* **Notre Dame, IN: University of Notre Dame Press, 1994.**

While the terms "Hispanic" and "Catholic" have often seemed synonymous, this book explores conflicts and concerns of the modern Hispanic Catholic.

**Fusco, Coco.** *English Is Broken Here: Notes on Cultural Fusion in the Americas.* **New York: New Press, 1995.**

Are Hispanics melting into the pot? This book discusses the successes and failures of Mexican Americans in merging into mainstream American society.

## CONTEMPORARY IMMIGRATION

**Brown, Peter G., and Shue, Henry, eds.** *The Border That Joins: Mexican Migrants and U.S. Responsibility.* **Totowa, NJ: Rowman and Littlefield, 1983.**

The immigration situation as it existed in the United States prior to the adoption of new immigration legislation is explored in this collection of essays.

**Browning, Harley, and de la Garza, Rodolfo O., eds.** *Mexican Immigrants and Mexican Americans: An*

*Evolving Relation.* Austin: Center for Mexican American Studies Publications, University of Texas at Austin, 1986.

A compilation of twelve papers delivered during a 1982 conference, covering a variety of topics dealing with Mexican immigrants and the emerging identity of Mexican Americans.

Cockcroft, James D. *Outlaws in the Promised Land: Mexican Immigrant Workers and America's Future.* New York: Grove Press, 1986.

This well-written survey of Mexican immigration history includes an analysis of the U.S. Immigration Reform Act, which was passed after the book was published. This act offered amnesty to illegal aliens and allowed growers to import foreign farmworkers.

Cornelius, Wayne A., and Anzaldúa Montoya, Ricardo, eds. *America's New Immigration Law: Origins, Rationales and Potential Consequences.* La Jolla, CA: University of California at San Diego, Center for U.S.–Mexican American Studies, 1983.

A 1982 symposium focusing on the Simpson-Mazzoli immigration bill is the setting for this collection of essays and edited commentary.

Ehrlich, Paul R., et al. *The Golden Door: International Migration, Mexico, and the United States.* New York: Ballantine Books, 1979.

This major study, with extensive footnotes, puts the Mexican immigration problem in its historical and cultural context, analyzing the effects of various possible policies.

Glazer, Nathan, ed. *Clamor at the Gates: The New American Immigration.* San Francisco: ICS Press, 1985.

A compilation of thirteen essays on immigration policy, social and political adaptation of immigrants, and on borders, sovereignty, and citizenship. For advanced readers.

**Jones, Richard C.** *Patterns of Undocumented Migration: Mexico and the United States.* **Totowa, NJ: Rowman & Allanheld, 1984.**

Compilation of essays by major scholars dealing with geographic migration patterns, with a focus on undocumented migrants. This volume may be of interest if your ancestors crossed the border illegally.

**López Castro, Gustavo.** *La casa dividida: Un estudio de caso sobre la migración a Estados Unidos en un pueblo michoacano.* **Zamora: El Colegio de Michoacán, 1986.**

A scholarly, well-documented case study of Gómez Farías, a town in Michoacán where 70 percent of the population has migrated at least once to the United States. Includes thirty-six statistical tables as well as an extensive bibliography. If your relatives happen to come from this town, this source may provide information on them. (Text in Spanish.)

## BIBLIOGRAPHIES AND REFERENCE WORKS

**Camarillo, Albert M.** *Latinos in the United States: A Historical Bibliography.* **Santa Barbara, CA: ABC-Clio, 1986.**

This reference work will lead you to many other titles dealing with the history of Latin American cultures in the United States.

**Clayton, Lawrence A., ed.** *The Hispanic Experience in North America: Sources for Study in the United States.* **Columbus: Ohio State University Press, 1992.**

This bibliographical work offers many additional sources for studying the history and cultures of Hispanics in the United States.

**Cordova, Gilberto Benito.** *Bibliography of Unpub-*

*lished Materials Pertaining to Hispanic Culture.* **Santa
Fe, NM: Bilingual-Bicultural Communicative Arts
Unit, Division of Instructional Services, State Dept. of
Education, 1972.**

> Letters, diaries, personal histories, and other unpublished
> materials like those listed in this book often provide the
> richest and most meaningful sources for family and social
> history. Speak to your librarian about locating this
> resource.

***Hispanic American Information Directory.* Detroit:
Gale Research, 1990.**

> This reference work provides information concerning
> organizations and institutions involved with Hispanic
> Americans.

**Kanellos, Nicholas, ed.** *Chronology of Hispanic American History.* **Detroit: Gale Research, 1995.**

————. *Reference Library of Hispanic America.* **New
York: Distributed by Educational Guidance Service,
1993.**

> These volumes can provide quick reference information as
> questions arise in your research. They are likely to be
> found in the reference section of your local library.

**Schon, Isabel.** *A Hispanic Heritage, Series III: A
Guide to Juvenile Books About Hispanic People and
Cultures.* **Metuchen, NJ: Scarecrow Press, 1988.**

> If you or a younger member of your family are looking for
> interesting but easy-to-read material about Hispanic cul-
> tures, consider the titles listed in this book.

**Tenenbaum, Barbara A., ed.** *Encyclopedia of Latin
American History and Culture.* **New York: Scribner,
1995.**

> This five-volume set covers the history and culture of

Latin America from the earliest Indian civilizations to the present day. Arranged in dictionary format.

**Valdivieso, Rafael.** *U.S. Hispanics: Challenging Issues for the 1990s.* **Washington, DC: Population Reference Bureau, 1988.**

As Hispanics become the largest minority in the United States at the end of the twentieth century, they are confronted by a variety of social and cultural challenges, many of which are explored in this book.

## MEXICAN AND MEXICAN AMERICAN ART

**Beardsley, John, and Beardsley, Jane Livingston.** *Hispanic Art in the United States.* **New York: Abbeville Press, 1987.**

This catalog of an art exposition of Hispanic artists in the United States puts Mexican-American art in the broader perspective of Latin American art. Introduction by the contemporary Mexican philosopher Octavio Paz.

**Drucker, Malka.** *Frida Kahlo: Torment and Triumph in Her Life and Art.* **New York: Bantam, 1991.**

The work of the Mexican artist Frida Kahlo continues to haunt and fascinate us today. In this biography, Drucker examines Kahlo's life and work.

**Eldredge, Charles C.; Schimmel, Julie; and Truettner, William H.** *Art in New Mexico, 1900–1945.* **Washington, DC: National Museum of American Art, 1986.**

For nearly a century, northern New Mexico has been an artist's haven. Although most of those artists have been Anglos, the chapter in this book called "The Hispanic Southwest" illustrates how they capture New Mexico's Hispanic lifestyle in their works.

**Fernández, Justino.** *Arte Moderno y Contemporáneo de México. Vol. 1, El Arte del Siglo XIX; Vol. 2, El Arte* *del Siglo XX*. **Mexico City: Universidad Nacional Autónoma de México, 1994.**

Since independence, Mexican art has been prolific and unique, a colorful and dynamic expression of Mexico. These two richly illustrated volumes explore Mexican art through two centuries. (Text in Spanish.)

**González, Nancie L.** *The Spanish-Americans of New Mexico: A Heritage of Pride*. **Albuquerque: University of New Mexico Press, 1967.**

This book provides insights into the unique culture of New Mexico, where Hispanics held on to their positions of influence in society.

**Gorodezky, Sylvia.** *Arte Chicano Como Cultura de Protesta*. **Mexico City: Universidad Nacional Autónoma de México, 1993.**

Illustrated with original works of many Chicano artists, this book examines how and why Chicano art and literature have been largely synonymous with protest, expressing the inherent frustration and conflict of reconciling the divergent elements of Mexican American culture. (Text in Spanish.)

**Orozco, José Clemente.** *Cartas a Margarita*. **Mexico City: Ediciones Eca, 1987.**

This book provides an intimate glimpse of José Clemente Orozco, one of the three great Mexican muralists of the twentieth century, through his letters to his wife. (Text in Spanish.)

**Paz, Octavio.** *Essays on Mexican Art*. **New York: Harcourt, Brace, and Co., 1993.**

English translation of essays on Mexican art by a twentieth-century Mexican philosopher who has prolifically explored what it means to be Mexican, beginning with his seminal work *Laberinto de Soledad* (*Labyrinth of Solitude*).

**Quirarte, Jacinto.** *Chicano Art History.* **San Antonio: University of Texas at San Antonio, 1984.**

Social protest and cultural self-expression are key elements in the history of Chicano art as it is explored in this selected group of readings.

**Rivera Barrientos, María del Pilar.** *Mi Hermano Diego.* **Mexico City: Secretaría de Educación Pública, 1986.**

This book is not only about art but about family history, that of the great Mexican muralist Diego Rivera as written by his sister. (Text in Spanish.)

**Stierlin, Henri.** *Art of the Aztecs and Its Origins.* **New York: Rizzoli, 1982.**

Extensive colored photos illustrate the art of this great Indian people, which forms so large a part of Mexican culture.

**Weismann, Elizabeth Wilder.** *Art and Time in Mexico: From the Conquest to the Revolution.* **New York: Harper & Row, 1985.**

Just as the concept of time is different and the past more present in Mexico, its art defies chronological characterization. Extensive illustrations.

**West, John O.** *José Cisneros: An Artist's Journey.* **El Paso: Texas Western Press, 1993.**

To peruse the illustrations and paintings of José Cisneros in this book is to explore the history of Mexican Americans and their place in the broader American society.

## MEXICAN AND MEXICAN AMERICAN MUSIC

**Dickey, Dan William.** *The Kennedy Corridos: A Study of the Ballads of a Mexican American Hero.* **Austin: University of Texas Press, 1978.**

*Corridos* (Mexican ballads) have for generations dealt with a variety of heroes, heroines, and antiheroines. These about John F. Kennedy are only a sample of the many that exist about contemporary people ranging from César Chávez to Selena.

**Herrera-Sobek, María. *The Mexican Corrido: A Feminist Analysis*. Bloomington: Indiana University Press, 1990.**

Female archetypes in traditional Mexican ballads offer insight into Mexican culture. Particularly interesting are the ballads dealing with the *soldadera*, the female soldier during the Mexican Revolution.

**————. *Northward Bound: The Mexican Immigrant Experience in Ballad and Song*. Bloomington and Indianapolis: Indiana University Press, 1993.**

*Corridos* (Mexican ballads) and popular songs are a rich expression of the tragedy, humor, irony, and joy of the Mexican immigrant experience. In addition to a text that discusses the subject in detail and many examples translated into English, this book has an excellent bibliography and discography.

**Loza, Steven. *Barrio Rhythm: Mexican American Music in Los Angeles*. Urbana and Chicago: University of Illinois Press, 1993.**

Nothing is more characteristic of Mexican American *barrio* culture than its music. This book traces the history of that music and has an excellent list of sample records.

**Marmolejo, Cirilo. *Historia del Mariachi en la Ciudad de México*. Mexico City: José Pablo Dueñas Herrera, 1994.**

This history of mariachi music in Mexico City illustrates the development and growth of this uniquely Mexican music style. (Text in Spanish.)

**Peña, Manuel H.** *The Texas-Mexican Conjunto: History of a Working-Class Music.* **Austin: University of Texas Press, 1985.**

The diversity and regional variety of Mexican American music is illustrated by this history of Texas-Mexican popular music. See the record list for excellent examples.

**Villanueva, René.** *Cantares de la Memoria: Recuerdos de un Folklorista.* **Mexico City: Grupo Editorial Planeta, 1994.**

A personal narrative of the history of folklore, another of the varied expressions of Mexican music. (Text in Spanish.)

## FILMS

*Alambrista!* **Directed by Robert M. Young, 1977.**

In an auspicious feature directorial debut, Robert M. Young directed this film about a naive young Mexican who chooses to slip across the U.S.-Mexican border in the hope of creating a better future for himself and his family. As an illegal alien, the protagonist, Roberto, is ruthlessly exploited and paid a pittance for his labor. A poignant and insightful look at the issue of illegal immigration in the United States and the attendant problem of social abuse as seen from the foreigner's perspective.

*The Ballad of Gregorio Cortez.* **Directed by Robert M. Young, 1982.**

The true story of Gregorio Cortez, a young Mexican who killed an American sheriff in 1901, and subsequently managed to elude a 600-man force during an eleven-day manhunt. Edward James Olmos stars as the mercurial Cortez.

*El Mariachi.* **Directed by Richard Rodríguez, 1992.**

On a budget of just $7,000, Rodríguez created this highly

acclaimed film about a young singing guitarist and his dangerous experiences in a small town where he is mistaken for an escaped convict. The sequel to this film, *Desperado* (1995), was also directed by Rodríguez and starred Spanish actor Antonio Banderas. Both films are for mature audiences.

### *Frida*. Directed by Paul Leduc, 1984.

A biographical portrait of Frida Kahlo, the Mexican artist and political radical. At the age of fifteen, Kahlo suffered a severe accident which prompted her to choose painting as the professional and personal focus of her life. Kahlo's art is itself highly autobiographical. In addition to tracing Kahlo's artistic development, the film details her relationships with the artist Diego Rivera and the Russian Communist leader Leon Trotsky.

### *Juárez*. Directed by William Dieterle, 1939.

The biography of Benito Pablo Juárez, the reformer and revolutionary leader who is today regarded as a national hero in Mexico. The film is set during the French Imperial rule of Mexico between 1864 to 1867, when the Austrian Archduke Maximilian von Hapsburg was installed as Emperor of Mexico by Napoleon III. Juárez led the Mexican people to a successful revolt against the puppet monarchy imposed on their country by Napoleon III, and subsequently resumed control of the presidency until his death.

### *La Bamba*. Directed by Luiz Valdez, 1987.

The musical biography of Richie Valens, the young Mexican American rock star who died in a tragic plane crash at the age of seventeen. The original music for the film was composed by Mexican American musician Carlos Santana and Miles Goodman.

### *Like Water for Chocolate*. Directed by Alfonso Arau, 1992.

Set in the early 1900s, this film explores the life of a young woman and her relationship to her family and to the cooking that shapes her life. Based on the novel by Laura Esquivel, written in the tradition of magical realism. For mature audiences.

### *Los Olvidados*. Directed by Luis Buñuel, 1950.

An unflinching portrayal of juvenile delinquency set in the slums of Mexico City. Struggling with poverty, physical and emotional hunger, peer pressure, and mutual opportunism, the youths depicted in the film are drawn to crime and violence as a form of entertainment and refuge. The adults in the story fail to set positive examples for the children and to give them the affection and trust needed to lead a better life. Buñuel injects scenes of his trademark surrealism into the cinematography.

### *Stand and Deliver*. Directed by Ramon Menéndez, 1987.

The story of a group of East Los Angeles *barrio* students who are inspired to pass the Advanced Placement Calculus Test by their demanding teacher, played by Edward James Olmos. Olmos is known for his real-life activism for Mexican and Latin causes. He played a central role in organizing a relief fund for Mexico City earthquake victims in 1985 and was an outspoken critic of governmental inaction during the Los Angeles riots of 1992.

### *Viva Zapata!* Directed by Elia Kazan, 1952.

Starring Marlon Brando and the celebrated Mexican American actor Anthony Quinn, this film traces the rise to power of Emiliano Zapata, the Mexican peasant who eventually became the President of Mexico. Like Pancho Villa in the north, Zapata was a revolutionary who led the insurgence against the dictatorship of Porfirio Díaz during the Mexican Revolution. The film was scripted by the American writer John Steinbeck. Quinn won an Academy Award for Best Supporting Actor his role as Zapata's brother.

# DOCUMENTARY FILMS AND VIDEOS

*Adelante Mujeres!* **National Women's History Project, 1992.**

A comprehensive examination of the history of Mexican American women. Focuses on their roles as family members, community activists, and contributors to American history.

*An American Story with Richard Rodríguez.* **PBS Video, 1990.**

Rodríguez, a young and critically acclaimed filmmaker, talks about growing up the son of Mexican American immigrants and negotiating his identity as a Mexican American and an American.

*Ano Nuevo.* **Cinema Guild, 1981.**

A look at the lives and working conditions of undocumented Mexican farmworkers at the Ano Nuevo flower ranch in San Mateo County, California. Depicts the struggle of a group of workers to join a union.

*Birthwrite: Growing Up Hispanic.* **Cinema Guild, 1989.**

Entertainer Cheech Marin hosts this examination of the Latino experience.

*Break of Dawn: A True Story.* **Cinewest Productions, 1988.**

The life story of Pedro J. González, a crusader for the rights of Mexican Americans in California during the Depression years.

*Chicana.* **Sylvian Productions, 1989.**

Mexican murals, photographs, prints, and documentary footage trace the traditional and contemporary roles of Mexican and Mexican American women from pre-

Columbian times to the present. Women's accomplishments as mothers, workers, activists, leaders, and educators, particularly in light of women's status in traditional Latino culture, are emphasized.

**"Los Mineros." PBS Video, 1991.**

Part of the PBS series, *The American Experience*. Tells the history of Mexican American miners in Arizona and their battle for fair labor practices in the copper industry.

*La Ofrenda: The Days of the Dead.* **Direct Cinema, 1989.**

A look at the tradition of the Days of the Dead celebration in both Mexico and the United States. In the first days of November, the dead are believed to come back for a visit, and they are greeted with offerings of favorite foods, flowers, and mementos.

*Recordar (To Remember).* **Other Pictures, 1989.**

Four generations of a Mexican American family in Silvis, Illinois, are documented using interviews, photographs, and home videos.

*Salt of the Earth.* **Independent Production Corporation, 1953.**

The struggle of New Mexican zinc miners to obtain better wages and conditions. Emphasizes the role of women in the struggle, as the miners' wives took up the battle themselves and left their husbands to care for the children.

*The Trail North.* **Cinema Guild, 1983.**

Anthropologist Robert Alvarez and his ten-year-old son retrace the steps of their Mexican ancestors who immigrated to the United States.

*Un Beso a Esta Tierra.* **Daniel Goldberg, 1994.**

This documentary features interviews with Jewish immigrants to Mexico. Now in their eighties and nineties, the interviewees describe how they overcame extraordinary odds to forge successful lives in Mexico. One of the interviewees worked at a synagogue for thirty years; another helped to found a Yiddish theater. The film is in Spanish with subtitles.

*Viva La Causa*. **Collision Course Video Productions, 1995.**

An introduction to the history of the Mexican American people. Covers European conquest of the Americas, World War II, the Chicano Movement, and other topics. Music and archival footage make for a lively presentation.

*Yo Soy*. **Cinema Guild, 1985.**

A look at the successes of Mexican Americans in business, education, labor, and politics.

*Yo Soy Chicano*. **Cinema Guild, 1972.**

Examines the challenges faced by the Chicano community and its responses to them.

## FICTION

**Anaya, Rudolfo A. *Bless Me, Ultima*. Berkeley: Tonatiuh-Quinto Sol International, 1972.**

A famous Chicano novel that recounts the relationship between a young boy, Antonio, and Ultima, a *curandera* or mentor. The novel is suggestive of the importance of oral tradition.

**Buss, Fran Leeper, and Cubias, Daisy. *Journey of the Sparrows*. New York: Dutton/Lodestar, 1991.**

The story of the intense and dangerous journey from Mexico to the United States undertaken by the fifteen-year-old protagonist María and her family. Once they arrive safely in Chicago, the family members confront the grim reality of their status as outsiders and the ever-lurking threat of being deported back to Mexico.

**Campobello, Nellie.** *Cartucho/My Mother's Hand.* **Austin: University of Texas Press, 1988.**

Two autobiographical novels about growing up amid the violence and turbulence of the Mexican Revolution. Narrated from a child's perspective.

**Castellanos, Rosario.** *The Nine Guardians.* **Columbia, LA: Readers International, 1959.**

One of the most important female Mexican novelists and poets of the twentieth century, Castellanos brings us this story set in the 1930s about the emerging new political order that began to take root after the Mexican Revolution. The narrator is a seven-year-old girl who witnesses the changes that occurred during the presidency of Lázaro Cárdenas (1934–1940), whose administration implemented many of the ideals of the Mexican Revolution embodied in the 1917 constitution.

**Castillo, Ana.** *The Mixquiahula Letter.* **New York: Doubleday, 1986.**

A novel told through letters that explores the friendship between two strong-willed women: Teresa, a writer, and Alicia, an artist. The letters offer a feminist perspective on the Mexican American experience and relate the two women's struggles to fight against the entrenched social expectations of their male counterparts. This novel, Castillo's first, was awarded the American Book Award from the Before Columbus Foundation.

————. *So Far From God.* **New York: Plume, 1993.**

A novel that traces the experiences of a Chicana family— a mother and her four daughters—over the course of two decades. The title of the book was inspired by a quote from Porfirio Díaz, the dictator during the Mexican Civil War who once described Mexico's spiritual and strategic location as "so far from God—so near the United States".

**Cisneros, Sandra.** *The House on Mango Street.* **Houston: Arte Público, 1984.**

Presented in a series of vignettes, this story recounts the experiences of a young Mexican American girl growing up in the *barrio* of Chicago. Esperanza Cordero faces the challenge of forging her identity within the parameters of a difficult social environment that offers few positive role models and leaders.

**Fuentes, Carlos. *The Orange Tree*. New York: HarperPerennial, 1994.**

This book is comprised of five novellas that explore Mexico's history in a highly inventive manner, fusing reality with fantasy. Delving into both Mexico's past and present, Fuentes analyzes the cultural clashes that have resulted from the interactions of the various peoples and civilizations of Mexico.

**Galarza, Ernesto. *Barrio Boy: The Story of a Boy's Acculturation*. Notre Dame, IN: University of Notre Dame, 1971.**

A fictionalized autobiography that traces Galarza's life from the days of his childhood in Mexico to his adult life in Sacramento, California, where he works as a migrant worker.

**Martínez, Max. *Schoolland*. Houston: Arte Público, 1988.**

An autobiographical novel set in Texas in the 1950s written from the perspective of a Mexican American teenager. Martínez candidly recounts his coming of age experiences, including his problems with prejudice.

**Paz, Octavio. *The Collected Poems of Octavio Paz, 1957–1987*. New York: New Directions Publishing Corp., 1987.**

The Nobel Laureate Octavio Paz is Mexico's foremost living poet. This collection features all the poems that Paz has published in book form since 1957.

**Rivera, Thomàs.** *The Migrant Earth.* **Houston: Arte Público Press, 1971.**

A series of fourteen vignettes detailing the experiences of Mexican-American migrant farmworkers. Various themes are explored, such as the exploitation of migrant workers, the emotional journey across the Mexican border to the United States, and the difficult adjustment to a new country and culture.

**Rulfo, Juan.** *Pedro Páramo: A Novel of Mexico.* **New York: Grove Press, 1994.**

A poignant novel about a son's search for the father he never met in the small town of Comala, where the memories and spirits of the dead come alive. The surrealism that Rulfo weaves into the narrative represents a break with the realism that largely characterized previous Latin American fiction and is a precursor of the style that has come to be known as "magical realism."

**Santiago, Danny.** *Famous All Over Town.* **New York: New American Library/Plume, 1983.**

A novel about a Mexican American teenager living with his family in Los Angeles. His sensitive nature clashes with the machismo expected of him by his father and his neighborhood street gang.

**Simmen, Edward, ed.** *North of the Río Grande: The Mexican American Experience in Short Fiction.* **New York: New American Library/Mentor, 1982.**

This is an excellent collection of short stories written by both Anglo and Latino authors that range from the nineteenth century to the present.

# Chapter 3
# How Do I Begin?

No matter how excited you are to start a new project, there is always that overwhelming feeling of wondering, "How do I begin?" With family history research, the answer is easy: Begin at home. You are the person who knows your own family best. Begin, too, by enlisting the help of family members, especially those who are older. After all, they are the real "experts" about your family history. They have lived through more of it than you have.

## The Preliminary Survey

As you begin compiling the history of your family, limit your focus to four things: 1) collect any family photographs, written information, or documents, 2) ask questions of family members, 3) check in your local Church of Jesus Christ of Latter-day Saints Family History Center for any records of your family members (See **Resources** for information on finding a Family History Center near you), and 4) check your library or an online library catalog for printed biographies or histories dealing with your family. These steps are usually called a preliminary survey, meaning a survey to be conducted before you undertake any research of your own. The preliminary survey will help you determine what is already known about your family. It might be more than you realize!

## Step One: Start at Home

What do your high school graduation diploma, your brother's draft registration, and pictures of your sister's wedding all have in common? They can all be classified as family memorabilia. The word "memorabilia" means "things

To acquire records and historical information about your family, you will need to find out where your ancestors lived. Many parts of Texas, like this neighborhood in El Paso in 1916, had large populations of Mexican immigrants.

worthy of remembrance," or things that give valuable information or tell about important times in the life of a family member. These are the types of items you want to look for in your preliminary survey. Ask your parents and family members where these kinds of items are kept. They may be in a special file or box. Attics are often favored places for keeping old records and documents. Below, we will discuss some of the things you might find:

> *Vital Records.* A vital record is a government or church record that documents a major event such as a birth, baptism, marriage, or death. Sometimes these are actual documents made when the event occurred, but they can also be copies that were made many years later. People often hold on to these kinds of records, because they are frequently needed as proof. For example, when you get your driver's license you will probably need a copy of your birth certificate to prove how old you are.
>
> A vital record from any country is a valuable find. Vital

records give specific dates and places for the events they record, information you can use as the beginning point for further research. A birth certificate, for example, lists the parents' names, thus providing you with more information for your family tree.

*Photographs.* Pictures make family history come to life. Once we have seen a photograph of a person, he or she becomes much more real to us. When you find old photographs, always check the back of the picture to see if the name of the person and either the date or place the picture was taken are recorded. This information makes the picture much more useful in piecing together the lives of your family members. If no information is given, perhaps an older family member can give you an idea of when the picture was taken. Remember in putting together your own scrapbooks to label carefully any photographs.

*Invitations or Announcements.* Probably the most common of these today would be wedding or graduation announcements. Did you know that in times past, death announcements were also common? You will be able to recognize them by the black border around the edges. In a Catholic country like Mexico there might also be announcements for first communions, baptisms, or *quinceañeras* (fifteen-year-old birthday/coming-out parties).

*Immigration and Naturalization Papers.* Paperwork is always involved in the process of leaving one country and traveling to live, work, and/or become a citizen of another. Passports are the most common immigration documents, but you might also find visas and citizenship or naturalization papers. Another document to look for is a work permit. For many years migrant workers who came into the southwestern United States needed to obtain one of these at the border in order to be hired.

*Legal Documents.* Did any of your family members buy or sell property, or make a will? The legal documents associated with these events can give you valuable insight about their lives. Keep your eyes open for contracts, tax bills, deeds, and mortgages.

Paperwork generated in the process of naturalization can provide you with important information and clues for your genealogical project. Above, Mexican-born Faustino López puts his naturalization papers in his pocket after becoming a U.S. citizen in 1941.

*Old Letters.* Think how much you could learn about a grandparent or other relative by reading one of their old letters. Daily events in their lives and problems they faced would seem much clearer if you could read about them from their own pen.

*Military Records.* It is likely that serving in the military was required for some of your male ancestors during their lifetimes. In fact, even women served in the Mexican Revolution. Mexican Americans have also served in U.S. wars. Among your family memorabilia may be a service record or award.

There are, of course, more possibilities than those listed above. As you learn about a family member and the activities in which he or she was involved, continue to ask yourself what type of documents might exist from that experience. For example, if he or she attended school, where would those school records be today? Many families make notes of birth, marriage, and death dates in a family bible. You should still confirm this information, of course.

A good way to begin collecting family memorabilia is to use a specific box or file and keep everything you find in the same place. Since you will be collecting these items from other family members, offer to make copies of any important documents or pictures that you find, and immediately return the original to the person who lent it to you. Remember that the things you are collecting are extremely valuable to other family members as well as to yourself. As the volume of your material grows, you can organize it into separate files for groups or individuals.

In your searching, try to reach as many of your relatives as possible. Aunts, uncles, or cousins may actually have a lot of the information you are looking for. It might be that the family keepsakes went to an oldest child, or the one who was most interested in saving things, not necessarily your parent or grandparent. If your relatives live far away, send a letter explaining your project and requesting their help in gathering information and memorabilia.

As you look for family memorabilia, remember that family members may know things they have never thought to tell you, simply because they didn't think you would be interested. Let them know of your excitement to learn about the family. Your interest may remind them of important information or stories they hadn't thought about for many years.

## Step Two: Talk with Family Members

Have you ever watched journalists on television as they interviewed celebrities and dreamed of what a glamorous and exciting career that would be? Well, here is your chance to give it a try. Some of the best family history details you can obtain will come as you talk with, or interview, older family members. However, just as professional journalists have spent hours in preparation for each interview, it is wise for you to plan your family interviews ahead of time. Let's suppose that you want to interview your grandmother. Here are some ideas to help make the experience a good one for both of you:

*Be Relaxed and Genuine.* If you are relaxed, your grandmother will be also. The more at ease your grandmother feels, the more she will feel like talking. In addition, she will find it easier to remember people, dates, and places—the very information you want to know. Let your grandmother know of your sincerity in wanting to know about your family. When she senses that, she will be more willing to cooperate.

*Record What Is Said.* Make sure that you have a way to record what is said during the interview. Don't trust your memory to keep everything clear as time goes by. A tape recorder or video camera would be best, since these record every detail exactly as it happens and allow it to be replayed in the future. If this is not available, however, take quick notes of important details by hand. The critical thing in this case would be to go back over your notes as soon as possible, and write out both the questions and the answers in greater detail. Even if you are recording the interview, you should still make written notes at the same time. This will help you to stay focused during the interview. Jot down new questions as you think of them.

*Know as Much as You Can About the Person Ahead of Time.* When we see a journalist on television interviewing a movie star or politician, we can be sure they have spent hours going through files of information about the person. This helps them ask insightful questions and lets the viewer learn as much as possible about the person who is being interviewed.

Your goal in interviewing your grandmother, or any other family member, should be the same. The more you know about her life before the interview, the more relevant your questions can be. For example, did any important historical events happen during her lifetime, or the lifetimes of her parents? Perhaps she came to the United States fleeing Mexican revolutionaries or with her family in search of work. What experiences did her family have as they settled into their new home? It is also possible that she, or her parents, were in Mexico during the Mexican Revolution. Did this affect any of her family members? Women as well as men served in the Mexican Revolution; she herself might have served for a period of time.

*Think Through Your Questions Ahead of Time.* Go into your interview prepared with some of the topics you would like to discuss and some of the things you want to know. This will help you to stay focused as the interview proceeds. Of course, there is no way to predict everything that the interview will cover, and some of your most exciting discoveries will undoubtedly come as you talk together. Remember that you want to learn as many names, dates, and places as you possibly can, since these are what will help you proceed on your own in tracing the history of your family.

*Avoid Controversial Topics.* Almost every family has some episodes that are negative or controversial to some family members. Since the goal of your interview, especially a first one, is to keep your grandmother relaxed and wanting

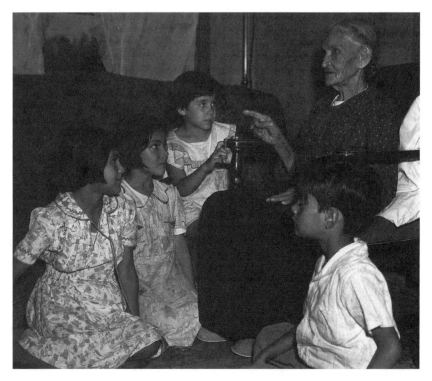

You can give life to your genealogical project by conducting interviews with older relatives who have witnessed many of the important events in your family's history. Above, 107-year-old Señora Placida Martínez de Amarillas talks with some of her great-grandchildren.

to share information with you, it would be wise not to bring up anything that might be hurtful. In this way an atmosphere of trust can be developed. With patience and time, perhaps painful topics can be broached, but it is best not to do so in a first interview.

*Keep the Interview Short.* If you stop the interview before either you or your grandmother grows tired, the experience will be a positive one for both of you and will leave room for the possibility of further talks. Be sure to thank your grandmother for her time and cooperation. Perhaps you could offer to make her a copy of either the tape of the interview or your later notes.

The following are some suggested topics and questions for a family history interview.

*Family and Self*
- What are the full names of all the members of your immediate family?
- When and where were you born? What are your mother's and father's dates of birth? Were they born in Mexico or in the United States? Which city or town are they from? When and where were they married?
- Please describe your childhood. Can you share any memorable anecdotes about your youth? What were your hobbies and interests?
- Can you tell me about your family life? Did you have a strict or liberal upbringing? Can you describe your family's financial situation? Did you have any particular chores or responsibilities as a child? Did you ever take any memorable family vacations? If so, can you describe them?
- Can you describe a typical meal at home? What kinds of traditional dishes did you enjoy? What kinds of etiquette rules or religious rituals did you observe during a meal?
- What was your school experience like? What kinds of themes, topics, or historical periods did your teachers focus on? How would you assess the educational system in Mexico?
- Did you attend college or a vocational school? What subject did you study? What kind of job(s) or apprenticeship(s) did you do before deciding upon your present-day career? Can you describe the education that your parents received? What occupations were your mother and father involved in? Did you ever feel any pressure from your parents to choose a particular career?
- Are you married? If so, where were you married and can you describe the wedding ceremony? How did you meet your spouse? What was a typical age for a man or woman to marry at the time you were married?
- What religious faith do you practice? Can you describe the role and significance that religion has had in your life? Do you own a family bible?
- Can you please share with me any Mexican myths,

legends, or folktales that you may have been told by your parents or relatives? What morals or values do you believe they are intended to illustrate?

- What Mexican national holidays do you celebrate? What significance do you attribute to these holidays? Have you ever participated in any traditional ceremonies, festivals, rituals, or rites of passage? If so, can you describe these events and their significance to you?
- Have you maintained any cultural and religious practices of your Mexican heritage? If so, which ones?
- Can you please show me any photographs, illustrations, diaries, momentos, medals, honors, or any other memorabilia that may be useful to me in understanding our family history?
- Do you know of anyone in the family who has already done genealogical research?

### History

- Do any historical events that occurred in your lifetime stand out in your mind? How did they affect your life? What were the chief concerns of your generation? What changes did your generation witness in such fields as politics, technology, or fashion?
- Were you or any of your relatives involved in the Mexican Revolution (1910–1928)? Were you or your ancestors part of the wave of emigration that Mexico experienced during the Mexican Revolution?
- Were you ever in the military? Did you or any of your relatives serve in the armed forces during World War I or World War II? If you fought in a war, can you describe your wartime experiences?

### Immigration and Contemporary Life

- The boundaries of Mexico have constantly shifted throughout history as a result of colonialism, wars, treaties, and the selling of land. Were your ancestors ever involved in the transfer of land between either Spain and Mexico or Mexico and the United States? Did any of your relatives become American citizens as a result of a transfer of land between Mexico and the United States?

- If you immigrated to the United States, when did this occur? What reasons lay behind your decision to leave Mexico to come to the United States? Can you describe the actual trip that you undertook from your homeland to the United States? What were your views of the United States before you came here?

- What kinds of challenges did you face when you came to the United States? How did you handle the difficult transition process? How quickly were you able to overcome the language barrier? What adjustments did you need to make to acclimate yourself to a new country and culture?

- What kinds of jobs were available to you? How would you describe your working and housing conditions?

- Did you live in a rural or urban environment? Was there a strong and supportive Mexican American community (a *colonia* or *barrio*) to ease your transition to a new way of life? Was the Mexican American community segregated from the Anglo-American community in the area where you lived?

- Were you, or was anyone you know, ever a victim of racism or discrimination? If so, can you recount any specific episodes of racism? Do you think that the problem of racial discrimination against Mexicans has improved, worsened, or remained the same since the time that you arrived in the United States?

- What are your views of contemporary immigration policies between Mexico and the United States?

- Have you or any of your relatives participated in the Chicano Civil Rights Movement? Do you believe that the efforts made by this movement have effectively secured equal rights for Mexican Americans?

- How has the experience of Mexican American women differed from that of men, in terms of job opportunities, cultural assimilation, and contributions to both the

Mexican American community and the larger American
society?

- Do you ever return to Mexico? Do you have relatives
there with whom you are still in contact?
- Who are your Mexican or Mexican American role models? Who are your favorite artists, writers, actors, musicians, and athletes?

Once the interview is over, be sure to put your tape or
notes in a safe place, such as the box or file of family memorabilia. Label it with the full name of the person you interviewed, your name, the date, and any other pertinent
information such as the place where the interview was held,
or others who may have been present.

In some cases the family member you wish to interview
may not live close enough for you to talk in person. In this
case the best option may be a telephone interview. Using the
concepts discussed above, you could speak with her over the
phone about the important events in her life.

If your relative is willing, you could also exchange information by letter. Be careful not to ask for too much information at a time, which might sound exhausting or
intimidating. It would be better to exchange several letters
over a period of weeks or months, asking for small amounts
of information in each. Better yet, if both of you have access
to e-mail, take advantage of this handy form of high-speed
communication.

Remember that in doing a preliminary survey your goal is
to talk with as many family members as possible. The more
information you get about events, the more you can rely on
the truthfulness of what you learn. Each person tends to
have his or her own perceptions of what has happened in the
past, and as years go by even the clearest memory tends to
fade. It is always reassuring to hear about an event from
more than one source and have the major facts agree.

As you begin the process of collecting family memorabilia
and talking at length with family members, you will undoubtedly make some exciting discoveries. As you learn

about the lives of family members, there will be stories of determination, humor, courage, and adventure. A woman in Texas learned that her great-aunt had made the four-hour train trip from Moucloug, Mexico, to Piedras Negras, Texas, riding on the top of a freight train. Because of the approach of a revolutionary army, huge numbers of people were leaving that part of Mexico, and the train was full. The train conductor took pity on her and agreed to let her ride on top of the train.

## Step Three: Search LDS Church Indexes

The Church of Jesus Christ of Latter-day Saints (Mormon Church) has done extensive microfilming of Catholic Church records, especially for Mexico. Because of their religious beliefs, the Mormons feel strongly about the value of family history research. The LDS Family History Library is the largest genealogical library in the world. It contains records on 2 billion people. The records they have filmed for Mexico (both religious and government records) are stored in Salt Lake City, Utah. However, you can easily access these records at one of their local Family History Centers. To find the nearest one, look in your phone book under the Church of Jesus Christ of Latter-day Saints or inquire of the main branch, listed in the **Resources** following this chapter.

At the Family History Center, an experienced volunteer will be available to help you. The first thing you will probably be shown is the *Family Search* program, which contains genealogical computer programs and databases. The possibilities for original research at the Family History Center are discussed in later chapters of this book. For your first visit all you will want to do is check what information may already be available about your family. There are two databases in *Family Search*: the Ancestral File, and the International Genealogical Index (IGI). Another database, the Social Security Death Index, is discussed later. A fourth database, the Military Index, will be of use to you only if you had a relative who died in the wars in Vietnam or Korea.

For years the Mormon Church has had a program to encourage people who have done family history research to submit copies of their work to a giant database called the Ancestral File. This allows researchers to share their findings with other researchers. The Ancestral File currently contains research on more than 20 million names. The 1994 edition contained relatively few Hispanic surnames, but as interest in Hispanic family history continues to build, these numbers will undoubtedly increase. Also ask for a copy of the pamphlet "Contributing Information to the Ancestral File" to see how easy it is to add your own family information as you find it.

The International Genealogical Index (IGI) is a collection of more than 200 million names from all over the world. More than 13 percent of these names are from Latin America, with the majority of these coming from Mexico. Check to see if the names of any of your ancestors are listed. If they are, either their birth date or marriage date will also be given, along with the location of this event and the names of their parents. Sources mentioned in the **Resources** at the end of this chapter can give you valuable help in using the IGI.

## Step Four: Look for Printed Biographies, Family Histories, and Surname Histories

While you are at the Family History Center, ask the volunteer to help you do a surname search in the Family History Library Catalog (FHLC). This is a catalog of the collection of nearly 2 million microfilms and books available through the LDS.

Check also in your local library for biographical dictionaries or genealogical encyclopedias containing your family name. Probably the most famous of these is García Carraffa's *Enciclopedia Heráldica y Genealógica Hispano-Americana*, listed in the **Resources** at the end of this chapter. It contains eighty-eight volumes published from 1920 to 1967, and covering the letters AA through URR. The first two volumes discuss heraldry (coats of arms), and the remainder discuss in alphabetical order by surname the noble and seminoble families of Spain and its former colonies, including Mexico. Also check on the Internet or at your local library for computer catalogs of libraries throughout the world. See your librarian for answers to research questions or to acquire materials via interlibrary loan, a service that is often free to library patrons. Your librarian will be happy to help you find the materials you need.

## Genealogical Research on the Internet

If you have access to a computer, a modem, and an Internet provider, you will also find the Internet useful for conducting genealogical research. Many organizations that specialize in genealogical research, such as the National Archives or the LDS library, have home pages on the World Wide Web. These pages (or web sites, as they are also known) allow you to access different types of data from your personal computer. You can browse data from census records or ship passenger lists from the comfort of your own home. You can request information that you cannot access from a home page by sending a message via e-mail. E-mail addresses for requesting information are often included at the bottom of home pages. You can also use the Internet to search the catalogs of libraries around the world.

Many smaller genealogical organizations also have web sites on the Internet. These pages almost always have links to other pages with related topics so that you can browse several different genealogical organizations quickly and easily. Publications and information about special events are often available online. A home page may refer you to online discussion groups, where you can meet other genealogical researchers—possibly even someone who could share valuable information with you. There are even sites that focus on a particular ethnic group or geographical area. Internet addresses for a few of the organizations that focus on Mexico are listed in the **Resources** at the end of this chapter.

## Where Did They Come from in Mexico?

As you trace your Mexican American ancestry, you will find yourself actually undertaking two tasks. The first is to trace your ancestors in the United States from the present back to the point when they crossed the Mexican border.

The most important question you need to answer during the American stage of your research is, "Where did my ancestors come from in Mexico?" You may be able to answer that question with documents found in your home search, or interviews with family members. If not, there are other valuable record sources in the United States that you can check.

The second part of your research may involve exploring your family history in Mexico. This is discussed in a later chapter.

Catholic Church records, especially marriage records, often give specific places of birth in Mexico. Church records are especially good sources because the priests who wrote the records were educated and aware of the geography of Mexico. They also knew the importance of giving specific information about parishes, which could help you to find the Mexican parish records of your ancestors. State vital records sometimes give similar, although often less detailed, information.

Look at the U.S. Federal Censuses from 1900, 1910, and 1920. If you can find any family members in one of these federal censuses, you can find out how long they had been living in the United States at the time the census was taken, whether or not they were naturalized, and other information about them.

Social Security Records can also provide useful data. The Social Security System of paying financial benefits to qualifying senior citizens started in the United States in the 1930s as a response to the Great Depression. By the early 1940s, the first benefits were being paid. In order to receive payments a person needed only to have worked for someone who had paid into the Social Security System. As a result, many Mexican Americans received Social Security whether they were citizens or not.

In order to receive Social Security benefits, an SS-5 form was filled out by the applicant. This form stated the names

Census records can provide you with many different kinds of information about your ancestors' lives. For example, you can find out the profession of your ancestors. Perhaps a member of your family owned and operated his or her own business, as did this pottery and toy shop owner in the Mexican quarter of Los Angeles.

of the applicant's parents as well as his or her birth date and place. If you think any of your relatives might have received Social Security benefits, you can send for copies of these forms. Write to:

Freedom of Information Officer
4-H-8 Annex Building
6401 Security Boulevard
Baltimore, MD 21235

It will cost less to order these forms if you know the Social Security number of the person you are researching. If you do not know this from home sources, you can check in the *Social Security Death Index* at your Family History Center. If the person died while receiving Social Security benefits, his or her name will be listed. Death certificates in the

United States often give the Social Security number as well.

Border Crossing Records from 1900 to 1940 are available on microfilm at the National Archives in Washington, DC, and possibly at field branches in El Paso, Texas, and Laguna Niguel, California. These records contain detailed information about everyone who crossed the border during this time period. You may even find a picture of the person. If your ancestors entered the United States at El Paso between 1903 and 1952, they may be among the 1.5 million immigrants whose names, ages, birthplaces, and last permanent addresses were recorded. These records are on microfilm at the LDS library or can be obtained by writing to:

Immigration and Naturalization Office
P.O. Box 9398
El Paso, TX 79984

If your ancestor became a naturalized citizen, you will want to check naturalization records. If your ancestor became a citizen before 1906, the process was handled in local courts in the city or county in which he or she lived, and the paperwork will be stored there. Check in the FHLC under the name of the locality to locate these records. After 1906 the process was handled by the Immigration and Naturalization Service. Inquire at the regional office in your area, or send a request to the national office:

U.S. Department of Justice
Immigration and Naturalization Service
425 I Street NW
Washington, DC 20536

The Alien Registrations of 1940 can be helpful when researching an immigrant ancestor. During the early 1940s, with another world war looming on the horizon, the United States started the process of registering aliens. (An alien is defined as a person living in a country of which he is not a

Border crossing records at the National Archives may give you information on your ancestors' passage from Mexico to the United States. The journey was often a difficult one. This family crossed the international bridge at Brownsville, Texas, in 1915.

citizen.) Although this was done in order to track people who had come from countries which were in political conflict with the United States, thousands of Mexican Americans were also registered. You can get copies of these records by writing to the Immigration and Naturalization Service at the address given above.

## Military Records at the National Archives

The National Archives has the largest collection of military draft and service records in the United States. At the Archives, military records are stored on microfilm, copies of which are available at major libraries with genealogical collections. The Archives also publish a booklet on researching military records entitled "Military Service Records in the National Archives." To request the booklet and order forms, write:

National Archives and Records Administration
Washington, DC, 20408

Because Mexican Americans have historically been well represented in the U.S. armed forces, military records are an excellent place to search for information on your ancestors. Above, a platoon of Mexican American servicemen takes a break from training at Fort Benning during World War II to enjoy an impromptu musical performance by fellow platoon members.

Records for some of the major wars in U.S. history are housed in the National Archives. You will probably have the best luck finding data on the Civil War (records from this war make up the bulk of their holdings) but you can also acquire information on other wars. For example, the Archives have a collection of military documents from the Spanish-American War, the War of 1812, the Indian Wars, and the Mexican War. Records for World Wars I and II, Korea, and Vietnam are restricted under privacy laws, but for additional information about records from these wars you can contact:

National Personnel Records Center
9700 Page Boulevard
St. Louis, MO 63132

Government records located at the National Archives can provide information about ancestors who may have worked for the U.S. government or participated in government programs. The Bracero Program of the 1940s enabled the legal importation of Mexican farmworkers, like the man pictured above, to address the shortage of agricultural labor caused by the World War II draft.

If you had male ancestors between the ages of seventeen and forty-five living in the United States in 1917 or 1918, they should appear in the World War I Military Draft Registration even if they were not then U.S. citizens. These records can be found in the FHLC in your local Family History Center under the headings "United States," "Military Records," "World War I," and "Selective Service Registration." The record will tell the place and date of birth and may even tell if your ancestor served in the army in Mexico.

All of the records discussed in this chapter will be helpful in locating family members living in the United States any time after 1847. Remember that up to the point where your ancestors crossed the border, you are doing American research. Before the point in time when your family crossed the border, you will begin doing research in Mexican sources, which are discussed in the last three chapters of this book. Remember that genealogists accept nothing as fact unless they have an official record of it. Use the information gathered from relatives as a starting point from which to begin your search for documents.

As you continue to learn new things about your family, no matter what side of the border they are on, you will undoubtedly make another discovery—you are well on your way to compiling your family history, and you're enjoying yourself.

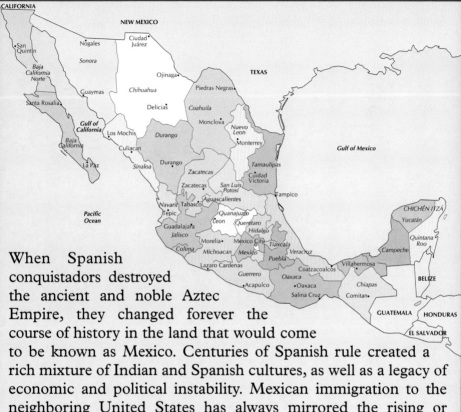

When Spanish conquistadors destroyed the ancient and noble Aztec Empire, they changed forever the course of history in the land that would come to be known as Mexico. Centuries of Spanish rule created a rich mixture of Indian and Spanish cultures, as well as a legacy of economic and political instability. Mexican immigration to the neighboring United States has always mirrored the rising or falling fortunes of Mexico itself. In the years following the Mexican Revolution, for example, waves of Mexican immigrants came to the United States to work in the fields and factories of the burgeoning western states. Not all Mexican Americans are the descendants of immigrants, however. In Texas, California, and New Mexico, Spanish-speaking families can claim many generations in areas that were formerly part of Mexico. Unfortunately, no matter where they have settled, Mexican immigrants and Mexican Americans have often faced discrimination because of their Mexican heritage. They have fought against social and political barriers with courage, vigor, and creativity. Mexican American writers, artists, activists, politicians, and scholars have channeled the energy of this struggle for justice into their work. The vitality and exuberance of their endeavors remind us that the Mexican American experience is a unique and vibrant part of the American cultural landscape.

Archaeologists say that the ancient city of Chichén Itzá was founded by the Maya in approximately 514 AD. Because it was abandoned by its original residents in 692 AD and reoccupied by another civilization in 928 AD, it displays multiple architectural styles. In 978 AD, the Mayan ruler Kulkulcán chose Chichén Itzá as the capital of his kingdom and made the Castillo, above, his principal temple. After his death, he became the patron deity of the city, and most of the structures were dedicated to him.

Picturesque Acapulco, on the Pacific coast of Mexico, was founded in 1550. It originally served as both a base for Spanish explorers and an important harbor for Spanish trade with the Philippines. The Spaniards constructed the Fort of San Diego there to protect the harbor from piracy. Today, Acapulco is the largest and most affluent resort city in Mexico.

This Mayan girl wears a traditional hand-embroidered blouse, reflecting the unique colors and patterns of her community in the highlands of Chiapas. The Maya of Chiapas were relatively isolated from the Spanish conquest of Mexico. Today they still maintain many of the traditions of their ancestors. In recent years, Mayan guerrilla fighters called Zapatistas have led an armed uprising against anti-Indian discrimination and exploitation in Chiapas.

Mexico City, the capital of Mexico, is home to the Paseo de la Reforma. The Reforma, as it is commonly called, is a wide boulevard that runs through downtown Mexico City and is studded by many *glorietas,* or traffic circles. *Glorietas* often contain circular gardens and historic monuments. Above, the gold-encrusted Angel of Independence, erected in one of the *glorietas* in 1909, gazes over Mexico City from atop a 130-foot-high Corinthian column.

Above, brightly costumed dancers celebrate Carnival in Tepeyanco, Tlaxcala. Carnival occurs just prior to the Catholic observance of Lent in late February or early March. It is traditionally accompanied by masquerades, pageants, and other forms of revelry —including singing, dancing, and playing of drums—that have their origins in traditional African beliefs and practices.

Every year on the first of November, people of Mexican heritage around the world celebrate *El Dia de Los Muertos*, the Day of the Dead. *El Dia de Los Muertos* is a festive occasion for families to remember the deceased. Celebrants decorate the streets with bright colors, papier mâché skeletons, portraits of their deceased loved ones, and candy skulls, such as this one being crafted by a Los Angeles resident.

Mexicans who have immigrated to the United States have brought with them a rich and beautiful culture, aspects of which continue to be embraced by younger generations. Above, Mexican American youths perform a traditional Mexican dance during a Catholic festival in San Elizario, Texas, near El Paso.

Nowhere is the blending of Mexican and American cultures more evident than in El Paso, Texas, located just across the Rio Grande from Ciudad Juárez, Mexico. El Paso has long been part of the primary trade and travel route through the mountains to the north. It is still an important way station for people traveling between Mexico and the United States, and its streets display a history of Mexican influence, such as this mural along Montana Avenue.

During periods of labor shortages in the United States, Mexican migrant workers have often filled a critical need, primarily as seasonal agricultural workers in California and the Southwest. This Mexican migrant worker loads a truck with grapes at a California vineyard. Mexican and Mexican American migrant workers have been active and often successful in fighting for their rights to receive livable wages, fair treatment, and decent working conditions.

Born to migrant-worker parents in New Mexico in 1930, Dolores Huerta went on to join forces with fellow Mexican American labor activist César Chávez in the fight for fair labor practices. The two founded the National Farm Workers' Association in 1962. Now known as the United Farm Workers Union (UFW), the organization was created to defend the civil and economic rights of agricultural laborers. Here Huerta addresses a news conference at UFW headquarters in Keene, California, after the death of Chávez in 1993. Above her is a portrait of the late Chávez.

Mexican immigrants and Mexican Americans have all too often been targets of racism and discrimination. They have fought these threats with dignity and courage. Above, the young son of a flower vendor attends a 1992 protest against police abuse of Mexican immigrants in New York City.

The Repertorio Español, founded in 1968, is an award-winning New York theater company that performs the Spanish-language works of Latino and Latin American playwrights. Above is a scene from the Repertorio's 1994 production of *Y se Armó la Mojiganga!* (*And the Carnival Erupted!*).

On March 31, 1995, fans from around the world mourned the death of twenty-three-year-old Mexican American music star Selena Quintanilla-Perez. Selena is credited with popularizing the *tejano* musical style, which originated in South Texas at the turn of the nineteenth century. *Tejano* is a fusion of polka music and traditional Mexican music and lyrics. Selena and her band, Los Dinos, took *tejano* music to new heights with their musical talent and charisma.

Los Angeles native Edward James Olmos has had a distinguished acting career, marked by such accomplishments as a 1986 Academy Award nomination for Best Actor for his work in *Stand and Deliver* and a 1995 Golden Globe Award for Best Performance in a Supporting Role in a Series for *The Burning Season*. Olmos is also known for his humanitarian work and social activism. He helped to organize a relief fund for the victims of the 1985 Mexico City earthquake and was an outspoken critic of governmental inaction during the Los Angeles riots of 1992.

Above, three generations of a Mexican American family in Laredo, Texas. Researching your Mexican American heritage is an opportunity to forge connections with your family members and celebrate your shared bond with the noble past of the Mexican people.

# Resources

## GENEALOGICAL BASICS

*AIS Census Indexes Resource Guide.* **Salt Lake City: The Church of Jesus Christ of Latter-day Saints, 1983.**

> Available in most Family History Centers, this is a guidebook to indexes of all pre-1870 United States Federal Censuses.

**Blea, Irene Isabel.** *Researching Chicano Communities: Social-Historical, Physical, Psychological, and Spiritual Space.* **Westport, CT: Praeger Publishers, 1995.**

> This book, through a multifaceted approach to understanding the Mexican American community, teaches the reader how to do research in an ethnic community.

**Doane, Gilbert.** *Searching for Your Ancestors: The How and Why of Genealogy.* **Minneapolis: University of Minnesota Press, 1960.**

> Includes chapters on finding information in cemeteries, county courthouses, government agencies, family papers, and churches. Contains appendixes on locating vital statistics, census records, and bibliographies.

**Dollarhide, William.** *Genealogy Starter Kit.* **Baltimore: Genealogical Publishing Co., 1994.**

> Dollarhide outlines his seven-step system for gathering essential genealogical facts: interviewing family members, contacting relatives, writing for death records, following up on death records, census searching, library searching, and state and county searching.

**Duaine, Carl Lawrence.** *With All Arms: A Study of a Kindred Group.* **Edinburg, TX: New Santander Press, 1987.**

An excellent and very extensive Mexican American family history.

**Eakle, Arlene, and Cerny, Johni.** *The Source.* **Salt Lake City: Ancestry, Inc., 1984.**

This collection of chapters by various experts in their field is a basic work for any family historian doing research in the United States. A second edition published in 1996 contains a chapter on how to trace Hispanic immigrants.

**Eichholz, Alice, ed.** *Ancestry's Red Book: American State, Country and Town Sources.* **Salt Lake City: Ancestry, Inc., 1992.**

Another basic work for a family historian wanting to locate local records in counties throughout the United States.

**Everton, George B., Sr.** *The Handy Book for Genealogists.* **Logan, UT: Everton Publishers, Inc., 1988.**

An excellent source for beginning family historians. The book contains a chapter on genealogical research in every state. The map and table at the back of the book will help you to locate the correct county courthouse from which to request records.

**García Carraffa, A.** *Enciclopedia Heráldica y Genealógical Hispano-Americana.* **AA-URR. Madrid: Nueva Impr. Radio, 1952–63.**

The first two volumes in this series discuss heraldry. The remaining volumes contain histories of thousands of surnames, with accompanying coats of arms. (Text in Spanish.)

**Garmendia Leal, Guillermo.** *Texas and Tamaulipas Founders.* **Vol. 1:** *Tamaulipas y Texas (1748–1770)*

*Villas del Norte.* Vol. 2: *Laredo, Texas (1757–1767).*
Vol. 3: *Cerralvo (1635–1760).* Vol. 4: *Cadereyta (1635–*
*1760).* Vol. 5: *Monterrey. Tomo I (Fundadores).* Vol. 6:
*Monterrey. Tomo II (Más de 2,000 familias y 250*
*Apellidos).* Vol. 7: *Diego de Montemayor (sus*
*descendientes).* Vol. 8: *Alonso de León (sus*
*descendientes).* Laredo, TX: 1992–1995.

These Ancestral File printouts record numerous Texan
and northeastern Mexican families. (Text in Spanish.)

**Gonzalbo Aizpura, Pilar (coordinadora).** *Familias*
*Novohispanas: Siglos XVI al XIX.* **Mexico City: El**
**Colegio de México, 1991.**

Use this book to explore prominent colonial-era Mexican
family histories. (Text in Spanish.)

**Gonzalez de la Garza, Rodolfo.** *Mil Familias de*
*Tamaulipas, Nuevo León, Coahuila y Texas, Vol. I &*
*II, and Appellidos de Tamaulipas, Nuevo León,*
*Coahuila y Texas.* **N. Laredo, TX: R. Gonzalez de la**
**Garza, 1980–81.**

These volumes set out the histories of more than 1,000
families from northeastern Mexico in the colonial era.
(Text in Spanish.)

**Greenwood, Val D.** *The Researcher's Guide to Ameri-*
*can Genealogy.* **Baltimore: Genealogical Publishing**
**Co., 1973.**

This is a classic on how to do genealogy in the United
States. It identifies the various types of genealogical records, where they are located, and how they can be used.

**Herrero Mediavila, Victor, and Aquayo Hayle, Lolita**
**Rosa.** *Indice Biográfico de España, Portugal e Ibero-*
*América.* **4 vols. New York: K. G. Saur, 1990.**

Certainly you can find someone with your surnames in
this index to biographical entries from over 700 volumes

of biographies and biographical dictionaries. Entries have been arranged in alphabetical order and filmed on microfiche. Available through your local LDS Family History Center. (Text in Spanish.)

**Hey, David. *The Oxford Guide to Family History*. New York: Oxford University Press, 1993.**

Contains great chapters on searching government records and church registries. Also has information on the origin of particular family names.

**Hilton, Suzanne. *Who Do You Think You Are? Digging for Your Family Roots*. Philadelphia: Westminster Press, 1977.**

Although you will want to acquire more recent sources eventually, this book remains a good place to start your genealogical search. It is written especially for young people.

***How To Use the U.S. Census*. Produced by The Family History Library, The Church of Jesus Christ of Latter-day Saints, 1993.**

This video, available at many Family History Centers, will take you step by step through researching with U.S. census records.

**Inglis, Douglas. "The Morelia Project in Mexico," in *Latin American and Iberian Family and Local History*. *World Conference on Records*. Vol. 9. Salt Lake City: The Church of Jesus Christ of Latter-day Saints, 1980.**

This article discusses the microfilmed records of the Catholic Church archdiocese of Morelia in Mexico, and the problems encountered with the cataloging of it in the FHLC.

**Jacobson, Judy. *A Genealogist's Refresher Course*. Baltimore: Clearfield Co., 1995.**

This book is not just for experienced genealogists; it is a treasure trove for genealogists with all levels of experience. Jacobson provides a large and detailed list of more than 100 kinds of genealogical information, from bank statements to health records. The information in the book is drawn from Jacobson's own genealogical experience.

**Kemp, Thomas J.** *International Vital Records Handbook*. **Baltimore: Genealogical Publishing Co., 1994.**

The applications for obtaining vital records vary widely from place to place. Kemp has compiled an up-to-date collection of vital record application forms for all fifty states and from countries around the world. Just photocopy the form you need, fill it out, and send it in. Kemp also provides advice on obtaining other documents, such as divorce certificates.

**Luebking, Sandra Hargreaves, and Szucs, Loretto Dennis.** *The Archives: A Guide to the National Archives Field Branches*. **Salt Lake City: Ancestry, Inc., 1988.**

Important record sources like U.S. censuses and immigration records may be found at the archives discussed in this volume.

**Mendirichaga Cueva, Thomas. Compiled by Edna Garza Brown.** *Surnames of Nuevo Léon: Botello y Buentello, Cavazos, Guerra, Hinojosa, Larralde, Mier, Sepulveda Zambrano*. **Corpus Christi, TX: Edna Garza Brown, 1989.**

This is another great example of Mexican American family histories.

**Neagles, James C.** *U.S. Military Records: A Guide to Federal and State Sources, Colonial America to the Present*. **Salt Lake City: Ancestry, Inc., 1994.**

Since the American Revolution, Hispanics have served in

the U.S. military. Consult this guide on how to locate military records.

**Nichols, Elizabeth L. "The International Genealogical Index," in** *New England Historical and Genealogical Register.* **CXXXVII (July 1983).**

An excellent discussion of the IGI and its use.

**Northrop, Marie E.** *Spanish-American Families of Early California, 1769–1850, Vol. II.* **Burbank, CA: Southern California Genealogical Society, Inc., 1984.**

**————.** *Spanish-Mexican Families of Early California, 1769–1850, Vol. I,* **2d ed. New Orleans: Polyanthos, 1976.**

These two volumes represent many hours of work identifying and compiling the families of early California.

**Parker, J. Carlyle.** *Going to Salt Lake City to Do Family History Research.* **Turlock, CA: Marietta Publishing Co., 1989.**

Consult this book when embarking upon step three of your preliminary survey. It will help you get the most out of the Family History Library's extensive collection.

**Platt, Lyman D.** *Spanish Surname Histories.* **Orem, UT: Automated Archives, 1984.**

Published on computer disk, this collection tells the origins of more than 1,000 Spanish surnames, and discusses people in the United States and Spain by those names.

**————.** *Una bibliografía de historias familiares de Latino América y Los Estados Unidos.* **Salt Lake City: Instituto Genealógico Histórico Latinoamericano, 1991.**

This collection lists more than 400 histories of Latin American families and where to find them. (Text in Spanish.)

Querexeita, Jaime de. *Diccionario onamástico y heráldico basco*. Bilbao, Spain: La Gran Enciclopedia Vasca, 1970–1975.

> If your surname is Basque, look it up in this book to find what it means and where in the Basque countries of northern Spain it originated. (Text in Spanish.)

*Research Outline: Arizona*. Salt Lake City: The Church of Jesus Christ of Latter-day Saints, 1993.

*Research Outline: California*. Salt Lake City: The Church of Jesus Christ of Latter-day Saints, 1993.

*Research Outline: Colorado*. Salt Lake City: The Church of Jesus Christ of Latter-day Saints, 1993.

*Research Outline: Louisiana*. Salt Lake City: The Church of Jesus Christ of Latter-day Saints, 1993.

*Research Outline: US Military Records*. Salt Lake City: The Church of Jesus Christ of Latter-day Saints, 1993.

*Research Outline: New Mexico*. Salt Lake City: The Church of Jesus Christ of Latter-day Saints, 1993.

*Research Outline: Texas*. Salt Lake City: The Church of Jesus Christ of Latter-day Saints, 1993.

> These research outlines will help you do research in the particular area in which your ancestors have lived in the United States.

Ryskamp, George R. *Hispanic Family History Research in the LDS Family History Center*. Riverside, CA: Hispanic Family History Research, 1993.

> A step-by-step guide to researching Hispanic names and surnames in the IGI and FHLC.

————. *Tracing Your Hispanic Heritage.* **Riverside, CA: Hispanic Family Research, 1984.**

Check chapters 1 through 3 for a detailed discussion on beginning Hispanic research, including the preliminary survey.

**Ugarte, José Bravo.** *Diócesis y Obispos de la Iglesia Mexicana (1519–1965), Colección México Heroico,* **no. 39. Mexico City: Editorial Jus, 1965.**

A history of the Catholic Church dioceses in Mexico. (Text in Spanish.)

**Westin, Jeane Eddy.** *Finding Your Roots: How Every American Can Trace His Ancestors—At Home and Abroad.* **New York: Ballantine Books, 1977.**

Covers everything from how to use the most fundamental records to writing and publishing family history. Contains a list of archives and stores that specialize in genealogical research. Includes information on Mexican American genealogy.

*Where to Write for Vital Records: Births, Deaths, Marriages, and Divorces.*

Order this booklet from the Superintendent of Documents, U.S. Government Printing Office, Washington, DC 20402.

**Wright, Norman E.** *Preserving Your American Heritage: A Guide to Family and Local History.* **Provo, UT: Brigham Young University Press, 1981.**

This excellent guide is another classic on researching family history in the United States.

**Zordilla, Juan Fidel, and Gonzalez Salas, Carlos.** *Diccionario Biográfico de Tamaulipas.* **Ciudad Victoria: Universidad Autónoma de Tamaulipas, Instituto de Investigaciones Históricas, 1984.**

Does your ancestry come from the Mexican state of Tamaulipas? If so, you will want to check this biographical dictionary for your surname. (Text in Spanish.)

## INTERVIEWING RELATIVES

**Allen, Barbara, and Montell, William Lynwood.** *From Memory to History: Using Oral Sources in Local Historical Research.* **Nashville, TN: American Association for State and Local History, 1981.**

An older relative's recollections can become the basis of a fascinating family history. Allen and Montell explain how to use oral sources to construct a history.

**Davis, Collom; Back, Kathryn; and Maclean, Kay.** *Oral History: From Tape to Type.* **Chicago: American Library Association, 1977.**

Consult this book for tips on interviewing, transcribing, and editing. Contains a glossary, bibliography, and illustrations of how to organize interviews.

**Deering, Mary Jo, and Pomeroy, Barbara.** *Transcribing Without Tears: A Guide to Transcribing and Editing Oral History Interviews.* **Washington, DC: Oral History Program, George Washington University Library, 1976.**

What do you do when your interviewee switches topics midsentence or makes a grammatical error? This book shows you how to deal with such issues when transcribing an interview. The authors also demonstrate how to use editing symbols when marking up the transcript of an interview.

**Harvey, Joanne H.** *The Living Record: Interviewing and Other Techniques for Genealogists.* **Lansing, MI: J. H. Harvey, 1985.**

This book provides helpful tips on how to obtain genealogical data by interviewing relatives.

**Schumacher, Michael.** *Creative Conversations: The Writer's Complete Guide to Conducting Interviews.* **Cincinnati: Writer's Digest Books, 1990.**

This book is written for professional writers, but the information in it will also be useful for the genealogist.

**Shumway, Gary L., and Hartley, William G.** *An Oral History Primer.* **Salt Lake City: Deseret Book Co., 1974.**

The authors guide you through the process of gathering oral history, from preliminary stages to transcribing interviews. The suggestions are simple and practical.

**Stano, Michael E., and Reinsch, Jr., N. L.** *Communication in Interviews.* **Englewood Cliffs, NJ: Prentice-Hall, 1982.**

The interviewing advice provided in this book can be applied to your family history interviews. The authors discuss how to prepare for an interview, how to communicate your questions clearly, and how to read your interviewee's verbal and nonverbal signals.

## INTERNET WEB SITES

**Everton Publishers Genealogy Page**
http://www.everton.com

This page contains information on getting started as well as specific information on ethnic, religious, and social groups. Includes an online edition of the genealogical magazine *Everton's Genealogical Helper* and provides links to archives, libraries, and other Internet resources.

**Genealogy Home Page**
ftp://ftp.cac/.psu.edu/pub/genealogy
http://ftp.cac.psu.edu/~saw/genealogy.html

By filling out the survey linked to this home page, you will be granted access to many genealogical links, allowing you to communicate with other genealogists, search new databases, and order genealogical software online.

## GenWeb

http://demo.genweb.org/gene/genedemo.html

This page is still under construction, but its goal is to "create a coordinated, interlinked, distributed world-wide genealogy database." Even in its incomplete form, GenWeb allows you to access all known genealogical databases searchable through the www.

## Hispanic Pages in the USA

http://www.clark.net/pub/jgbustam/heritage/heritage.html

This site offers information on topics relating to Hispanic individuals, countries, history, and culture. Of particular interest is the link to the Famous Hispanics home page, which lists famous individuals in categories such as painters, scientists, writers, musicians, and Nobel Prize winners.

## LatinoWeb

http://www.latinoweb.com/favision

LatinoWeb is a "virtual information center" for Latino businesses, nonprofit organizations, and the Latino community. It provides a forum for the private, nonprofit, and public sectors to exchange information. From this web site you can access information on books, art, music, sports, upcoming events, and many other topics.

## LDS Research Guides

ftp://hipp.etsu.edu/pub/genealogy

This site focuses on the Research Outline Guides produced by the Family History Library in Salt Lake City. Subjects include getting started, frequently asked genealogy questions, and techniques for photograph dating.

## Mexican American Research Guide

http://www.usc.edu/Library/Ref/Ethnic/mex_main.html

This is a general guide to library resources in the University Library at the University of Southern California. Categories you can search include Mexican American Literature, Mexican American Art, Politics and Mexican Americans, Dictionaries and Encyclopedias, Directories, Biographical Sources, Indexes, Magazines and Journals, Videorecordings, and links to other Mexican American resources on the Internet.

**National Archives and Records Administration**
gopher://gopher.nara.gov
http://www.nara.gov

NARA is the government agency responsible for managing the records of the federal government. Through this page you can find the location and business hours for regional archives or access information on finding and using particular government documents.

**U.S. Census Bureau**
ftp://gateway.census.gov
http://www.census.gov

From this site you can access statistics about population, housing, economy, and geography as compiled by the U.S. Department of Commerce Bureau of the Census. You can also do specific word searches according to subject or geographic location.

# Chapter 4
# Charts and Computers: Organizing What You Find

Up to this point you have been concerned only about collecting items that will help in putting together your family history. As your box or container fills with valuable documents and photographs, however, you will probably find it cumbersome to sort through the entire contents when you need any family information, such as the date somebody was married or the number of children in your uncle's family. It will soon make more sense to have a place where things are written down so you can easily find the names and dates you are looking for.

## Pedigree Charts

A pedigree chart like the one pictured on page 102 is the first tool you will want in organizing the facts you have found so far and will continue to find. Pedigree charts are available in any Family History Center or any bookstore that sells genealogy supplies.

Take a minute to examine the fictitious pedigree chart on page 102. The person who is filling out the chart, Angelina Maria Cruz Martin, puts her own information in the spaces on the far lefthand side, under #1. Note that there is a space for your name, and below that your birth date and the place where you were born. In order to make the information as complete as possible, you would use all of your given names and your complete surname. Also notice that in the example the surname is capitalized, making it easy to distinguish from the given name. For example, the name Martin is a surname here, and not a given name.

# Pedigree Chart

Name of Compiler _____

Address _____

City, State _____

Date _____

Person No.1 on this chart is the same person as No._____ on chart No._____.

Chart No._____

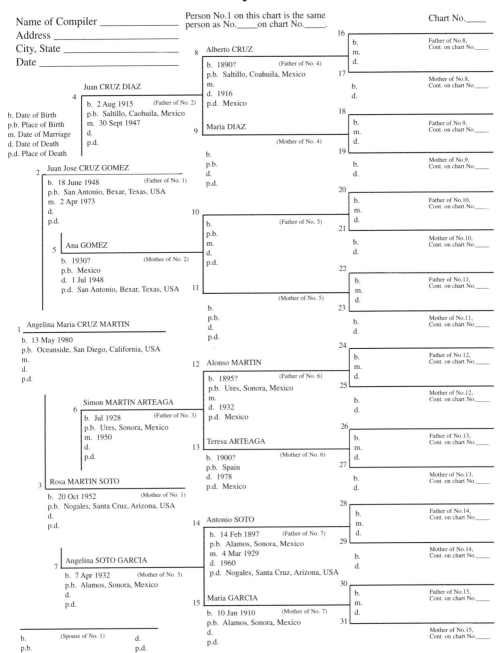

**1** Angelina Maria CRUZ MARTIN
b. 13 May 1980
p.b. Oceanside, San Diego, California, USA
m.
d.
p.d.

b. Date of Birth
p.b. Place of Birth
m. Date of Marriage
d. Date of Death
p.d. Place of Death

**2** Juan Jose CRUZ GOMEZ
b. 18 June 1948          (Father of No. 1)
p.b. San Antonio, Bexar, Texas, USA
m. 2 Apr 1973
d.
p.d.

**3** Rosa MARTIN SOTO
b. 20 Oct 1952          (Mother of No. 1)
p.b. Nogales, Santa Cruz, Arizona, USA
d.
p.d.

**4** Juan CRUZ DIAZ
b. 2 Aug 1915          (Father of No. 2)
p.b. Saltillo, Caohuila, Mexico
m. 30 Sept 1947
d.
p.d.

**5** Ana GOMEZ
b. 1930?          (Mother of No. 2)
p.b. Mexico
d. 1 Jul 1948
p.d. San Antonio, Bexar, Texas, USA

**6** Simon MARTIN ARTEAGA
b. Jul 1928          (Father of No. 3)
p.b. Ures, Sonora, Mexico
m. 1950
d.
p.d.

**7** Angelina SOTO GARCIA
b. 7 Apr 1932          (Mother of No. 3)
p.b. Alamos, Sonora, Mexico
d.
p.d.

**8** Alberto CRUZ
b. 1890?          (Father of No. 4)
p.b. Saltillo, Coahuila, Mexico
m.
d. 1916
p.d. Mexico

**9** Maria DIAZ
          (Mother of No. 4)
b.
p.b.
d.
p.d.

**10**
          (Father of No. 5)
b.
p.b.
m.
d.
p.d.

**11**
          (Mother of No. 5)
b.
p.b.
d.
p.d.

**12** Alonso MARTIN
b. 1895?          (Father of No. 6)
p.b. Ures, Sonora, Mexico
m.
d. 1932
p.d. Mexico

**13** Teresa ARTEAGA
b. 1900?          (Mother of No. 6)
p.b. Spain
d. 1978
p.d. Mexico

**14** Antonio SOTO
b. 14 Feb 1897          (Father of No. 7)
p.b. Alamos, Sonora, Mexico
m. 4 Mar 1929
d. 1960
p.d. Nogales, Santa Cruz, Arizona, USA

**15** Maria GARCIA
b. 10 Jan 1910          (Mother of No. 7)
p.b. Alamos, Sonora, Mexico
d.
p.d.

**16**
Father of No.8,
Cont. on chart No._____
b.
m.
d.

**17**
Mother of No.8,
Cont. on chart No._____
b.
d.

**18**
Father of No.9,
Cont. on chart No._____
b.
m.
d.

**19**
Mother of No.9,
Cont. on chart No._____
b.
d.

**20**
Father of No.10,
Cont. on chart No._____
b.
m.
d.

**21**
Mother of No.10,
Cont. on chart No._____
b.
d.

**22**
Father of No.11,
Cont. on chart No._____
b.
m.
d.

**23**
Mother of No.11,
Cont. on chart No._____
b.
d.

**24**
Father of No.12,
Cont. on chart No._____
b.
m.
d.

**25**
Mother of No.12,
Cont. on chart No._____
b.
d.

**26**
Father of No.13,
Cont. on chart No._____
b.
m.
d.

**27**
Mother of No.13,
Cont. on chart No._____
b.
d.

**28**
Father of No.14,
Cont. on chart No._____
b.
m.
d.

**29**
Mother of No.14,
Cont. on chart No._____
b.
d.

**30**
Father of No.15,
Cont. on chart No._____
b.
m.
d.

**31**
Mother of No.15,
Cont. on chart No._____
b.
d.

b.          (Spouse of No. 1)          d.
p.b.                                    p.d.

Note also the consistency in writing dates. If your birthday was June 12, 1979, you would write it as 12 June 1979 on the pedigree chart. It may seem quicker to write the date in numbers only, but in Mexico the day is placed before the month, whereas in the United States the month is placed before the day. Therefore, when you see the date 6/7/79 you could not be certain whether the person filling out the chart meant June 7, 1979, or July 6, 1979.

Next, note the way place names are given. Remember that your goal in filling out a pedigree chart is to give as brief and accurate a description as you can. For place names in the United States, put the city first, followed by the county, the state, and the country (San Antonio, Bexar, Texas, USA). Place names in Mexico are written with the city followed by the state and then the country (Saltillo, Coahuila, Mexico). Standard abbreviations for states are fine, as long as their meaning would be clear to another reader.

At first, the addition of the county for U.S. place names and the state for Mexican place names may seem like a lot of extra work. However, you will find it helpful in locating places clearly. For example, San Antonio could be the city in Bexar County, Texas, or a small town in the Mexican state of Coahuila. Without a state mentioned, Saltillo, Mexico, could be either the Saltillo in the state of Puebla, or the Saltillo in the state of Coahuila.

After filling in the information about yourself, fill in your father's name. This is called the paternal line. Note that the father's information is always shown on the line above the person who is the child, and the mother's information is always shown on the line below. Using the same rules regarding names, dates, and place names, fill in the information that you know about your father. Then, following the same guidelines, fill in the lines about your mother. This is called the maternal line. Then add the information about your four grandparents.

Now, look again at the pedigree chart on page 102. Do you see the number 1 by the first name on the left-hand side? This is called the Sosa number. If you were filling out a pedigree chart for yourself, you would be number one. Your father would be number two, and your mother would be number three. In other words, your father's number is double the number for you, and your mother's number is double your number plus one. As you study the pedigree chart, you will find that this system continues no matter how far back you go in time. The child's number times two is the number of the father. The child's number times two, plus one, is the number of the mother. Within a short time you will find that working with the Sosa system will be natural and helpful to you.

Notice that not all of the lines in the pedigree chart in our example are filled in. It is likely that not all of the lines in your chart will be completely filled in, either. Do not be discouraged if this is the case. Think of your pedigree chart as a way to let yourself know the information that you have so far, and the direction that you want to take next. If you are unsure of a date or location, put a question mark next to it. This will remind you that the date is not exact.

## Family Group Sheets

As you look at a pedigree chart, no matter how complete, you will quickly realize that a lot of information about the families you are researching is not given. For example, there is no place to list children, their birth dates, their spouses, their dates of marriage, or their death. All of this information goes on a family group sheet. A family group sheet allows you to list all of the vital information (births, marriages, deaths) about each member of a family.

Family group sheets can be bought in any Family History Center or bookstore that sells genealogical supplies. To begin your own research, you should fill out three family group sheets, one for your own family, one for the family of your father, and one for the family of your mother.

Begin by filling out the family group sheet for your own family. See page 105 for an example of a family group sheet that has been filled out. Using the same guidelines that were used in working with the pedigree chart, fill out the informa-

# Family Group Record - 1

## Husband - Juan Jose CRUZ GOMEZ

| | |
|---|---|
| Born (day month year) | Place |
| 18 Jun 1948 | San Antonio, Bexar, Texas, USA |
| Christened | Place |
| | |
| Died | Place |
| | |
| Buried | Place |
| | |
| Married | Place |
| 2 Apr 1973 | Los Angeles, Los Angeles, California, USA |
| Husband's father | |
| | Juan CRUZ DIAZ |
| Husband's mother | |
| | Ana GOMEZ |

## Wife - Rosa MARTIN SOTO

| | |
|---|---|
| Born (day month year) | Place |
| 20 Oct 1952 | Nogales, Santa Cruz, Arizona, USA |
| Christened | Place |
| 25 Oct 1952 | Nogales, Santa Cruz, Arizona, USA |
| Died | Place |
| | |
| Buried | Place |
| | |
| Wife's father | |
| | Simon MARTIN ARTEAGA |
| Wife's mother | |
| | Angelina SOTO GARCIA |

## Children List each child (whether living or dead) in order of birth.

### Sex-M    John Joseph CRUZ MARTIN

| | |
|---|---|
| Born (day month year) | Place |
| 20 Jan 1975 | Los Angeles, Los Angeles, California, USA |
| Christened | Place |
| 15 Feb 1975 | Los Angeles, Los Angeles, California, USA |
| Died | Place |
| | |
| Spouse | |
| | |
| Married | Place |

### Sex-F    Angelina Maria CRUZ MARTIN

| | |
|---|---|
| Born (day month year) | Place |
| 13 May 1980 | Oceanside, San Diego, California, USA |
| Christened | Place |
| 15 Jun 1980 | Oceanside, San Diego, California, USA |
| Died | Place |
| | |
| Spouse | |
| | |
| Married | Place |

tion about your parents. Next, list all of your brothers and sisters (these are called siblings) in the order they were born, along with the date and place of their birth. (Be sure to include yourself.) Remember any brothers or sisters who may have died, even if they died at the time of their birth. You will see that there is a place to list any deaths. If you have brothers or sisters who are married, write down the dates of their marriages and the names of their spouses. Some of them may have children, but there is no place for that information, as it would become too confusing. You can make a separate family group sheet for their families later.

## Computer Programs

The computer has become a way of life in our generation, and it has made its impact on family history as well. As you begin researching your family history, you may find the computer helpful in organizing your information. The most commonly used family history computer program is called Personal Ancestral File (PAF). It is available through the Church of Jesus Christ of Latter-day Saints at a cost of under forty dollars, which makes it one of the most affordable programs available. When you visit your Family History Center, ask one of the volunteers to show you the PAF program and how it works. It is even possible to load your own information into it without charge if you are interested. (The completed pedigree chart and family group sheet used as examples in this chapter were made using a PAF form.)

Although PAF has many advantages, it nevertheless has certain weaknesses, such as name searches and entering notes. You can solve these problems by using shareware available through a PAF User's Group. Ask your Family History Center librarian about a group near you.

Other commercial programs are available that can give you capabilites not found in PAF. In the **Resources** is a list of a few of them, with the addresses of their manufacturers. No matter which program you choose, be sure that it has GEDCOM capabilities. That means that the program can transfer data to other programs, or input data from other files such as those found in the Family Search program at your Family History Center. The *National Genealogical Society Newsletter* has a Computer Interest Group section that can give you updated information about the various programs available. No matter which computer program you ultimately choose, you will be happy with the amazing help it provides in organizing the growing database of your family history.

# Resources

## FAMILY GROUP SHEETS AND PEDIGREE CHARTS

**Evelyn Spears Family Group Sheet Exchange**
**East 12502 Frideger**
**Elk, WA 99009**

> A service that provides previously researched family group sheets from a catalog of about 14,000. The charge for each surname you request is about ten dollars.

**Everton Publishers, Inc.**
**P.O. Box 368**
**Logan, UT 84321**

> Everton publishes genealogical books and forms. Write for a catalog.

**Genealogical Center, Inc.**
**International Family Group Sheet Exchange**
**P.O. Box 17698**
**Tampa, FL 33682**

> You can write and request their catalog of over 8,000 surnames. The service charges thirty cents per page of researched data, and studies can range from ten to 300 pages.

**National Genealogical Society**
**4527 17th Street North**
**Arlington, VA 22207-2363**

> The National Genealogical Society sells a variety of forms, research aids, and books. Write to request a membership brochure and price list. This family group sheet is considered to be the best available.

**Ryskamp, George R.** *Finding Your Hispanic Roots.* **Baltimore: Genealogical Publishing Co., 1996.**

Chapter 3 contains tips for using computers as well as pedigree charts and family group sheets in tracing your Hispanic ancestors.

**————.** *Tracing Your Hispanic Heritage.* **Riverside, CA: Hispanic Family History Research, 1984.**

Chapter 3 explains in detail the use of pedigree charts and family group sheets in Hispanic family history research.

**Schreiner-Yantis Family Group Sheets**
**GBIP**
**6818 Lois Drive**
**Springfield, VA 22150**

Designed by Netti Schreiner-Yantis, these family group sheets, pedigree charts, and other forms are popular among genealogists. Write for a catalog and price list.

## COMPUTER GENEALOGY

**Clifford, Karen.** *Genealogy and Computers for the Complete Beginner,* **2d ed. Baltimore: Clearfield Co., 1995.**

A step-by-step guide for the beginner in both genealogy and computers.

**————.** *Genealogy and Computers for the Determined Researcher,* **2d ed. Baltimore: Clearfield Co., 1995.**

The advice in this book is aimed at the genealogist who is gaining experience.

**————.** *Genealogy and Computers for the Advanced Researcher,* **2d ed. Baltimore: Clearfield Co., 1995.**

Consult this guide when you have reached a point of being adept and comfortable when using your computer to perform genealogical tasks.

**Crowe, Elizabeth Powell.** *Genealogy Online: Researching Your Roots.* **New York: Windcrest/McGraw Hill, 1995.**

> This book will introduce you to the many research possibilities available through the Internet.

**Nichols, Elizabeth L.** *The Genesis of Your Genealogy: Step-by-Step Instruction for the Beginner in Family History,* **3d ed. Salt Lake City: Family History Educators, 1992.**

> The third edition of this basic book on beginning research is completely updated and revised to include the use of computers.

**Pence, Richard A.** *Computer Genealogy: A Guide to Research Through High Technology.* **Salt Lake City: Ancestry, Inc., 1991.**

> Although somewhat dated, this is still the classic work on using computers in genealogical research.

**Przecha, Donna, and Lowrey, Joan.** *Guide to Genealogy Software.* **Baltimore: Genealogical Publishing Co., 1993.**

> A review of 155 genealogy programs, designed to give the family history researcher an evaluation of genealogy software on the market today.

*Reference Manual, Personal Ancestral File, Release 2.31.* **Salt Lake City: The Church of Jesus Christ of Latter-day Saints, 1994.**

> This is the user's manual that comes with the PAF program when you buy it.

## GENEALOGICAL SOFTWARE PROGRAMS

**Ancestral Quest**
**Incline Software**
**P.O. Box 17788**

Salt Lake City, UT 84117-0788
800-825-8864

Brother's Keeper 5.2
John Steed
6907 Childsdale Road
Rockford, MI 49341
616-866-9422

Family Connections and Family Roots
Quinsept, Inc.
P.O. Box 216
Lexington, MA 02173
800-637-7668

Family Origins 2.5 for DOS, Windows
Parsons Technology
One Parsons Drive
P.O. Box 100
Hiawatha, IA 52233-0100
800-223-6925 (orders)

Family Tree Maker 3.0
Banner Blue Software
P.O. Box 7865
Fremont, CA 94537
510-794-6850

MacRoots II
Itasca Softwords
P.O. Box 427
Bagley, MN 56621-0427
218-785-2745

The Master Genealogist 1.0
Bob Velke
Wholly Genes Software
6868 Ducketts Lane

Elk Ridge, MD 21227
410-796-2447

Personal Ancestral File 2.3
Church of Jesus Christ of Latter-day Saints
Salt Lake Distribution Center
1999 West 1700 South
Salt Lake City, UT 84101
800-537-5950

ROOTS III or ROOTS IV
COMMSOFT, Inc.
P.O. Box 310
Windsor, CA 95492-0310
800-327-6687

# Chapter 5
# Working with Mexican Documents

The process of making your preliminary survey helped you become better acquainted with family members both alive and deceased. Now that you have started your family history, you can see how collecting family memorabilia and staying in touch with relatives is something you will want to continue throughout your life. It is called a preliminary survey only because it lets researchers know where they need to begin in doing their own family history. One of the most important goals of your preliminary survey was to determine where in Mexico your family came from. The smaller an area you can pinpoint, the better your chances will be for doing successful research in the future.

## The Locality Analysis

Once you have determined the specific place your ancestors came from in Mexico, you can locate the town on a map and find books that tell about it. This step is called a locality analysis. Once again you will want to head for your local library or the library of a nearby university. This time you will go to the map section and check the following sources:

> *Atlases and Maps.* An atlas is simply a book of maps. An excellent atlas for Mexico, *Nuevo Atlas Porrúa de la República Mexicana,* is listed in the **Resources**. Look up the locality where your ancestors lived. As you do so, think about what life would be like in that town. Is it in the mountains or is it flat? Would there have been a lot of trees? What was the water source? Was there a lot of rainfall or was it a dry area? What types of crops do you think they could have grown? Was the town small or

Perhaps your research will eventually take you to Mexico to visit the village of your ancestors and to gain firsthand knowledge of the culture and people of your ancestral country.

large? If small, how far away was the nearest town of any size?

An atlas may not be able to answer all of your questions. However, other reference works can give you more information.

*Gazetteers* are "dictionaries" of place names with a small amount of information to identify and help locate towns. A gazetteer provides geographical subdivisions smaller than a parish or a municipality. It also lists other features such as rivers and mountains. Most gazetteers give the latitude and longitude of the places listed.

*Geographical Dictionaries.* A geographical dictionary lists all the towns and hamlets (small villages) in a country, both those existing today and those that existed in the past. Each entry gives a brief historical sketch of the town.

*Historical Atlases, Maps, and Materials.* This category is for reference works printed before 1900 but still available today, or those that were written specifically to deal with geography of a past time period.

*Ecclesiastical Guides and Directories.* An ecclesiastical guide indicates the parishes, seminaries, and convents that make up a Catholic Church diocese. This information is extremely valuable because it will lead you to parish records.

*Local histories.* As the name implies, these are histories that deal entirely with a particular town or region, found both as books and as articles in periodicals. Scholarly historical journals such as *The Americas* and *Hispanic American Historical Review* are particularly valuable. These do not help in locating exact places, but they can be extremely valuable in helping to understand the history of that locality and especially to trace its jurisdictional changes.

These are the six major categories of books that can be valuable in completing a locality analysis. In the **Resources** following this chapter we will describe the general functioning of each category. In parentheses at the end of each entry is the code FHL and/or BYU with a call number, indicating that the work is available at the Family History Library or in the map collection at Brigham Young University in Provo, Utah. The latter is representative of what might be available at other universities. Those entries followed by FHL and a film number can be ordered for examination at your local Family History Center.

## Finding Birth, Marriage, and Death Records: Civil Registers

Completing your locality analysis will give you the information necessary to begin finding actual birth, marriage, and death records from Mexico. These documents can be found in civil registers and parish records. Parish records are discussed in the next section.

Civil registers contain documents made by the government to record births, marriages, and deaths. To research in civil registers you need to know the *municipio* (city or municipality) where your ancestor lived. Many civil registers in Mexico have been converted to microfilm, and a search of the Family History Library Catalog in your local Family History Center will reveal whether or not microfilmed records from the locality you are searching for are available. Look under the name of the *municipio*.

Records dating from 1900 to the present have usually not been filmed, for reasons of privacy. If the dates for the person you are researching would fall into these years, you can write to the state office of the civil register requesting the documents. Addresses of these offices as well as suggestions for writing letters to Mexico are included at the end of this chapter.

A birth entry from a civil register would include the following information: the given names and surnames of the child; the hour, day, month, and year that the baby was born; the town in which the event took place; and the street address of the house or hospital where the baby was born. In addition, the parents' full names are given, along with the places of their births, marital status, residence, professions, and sometimes dates of birth. This same information is usually given for the grandparents as well. If any of these people are deceased, that information will also be given. The entry usually ends with the names of witnesses. They were not necessarily present at the birth of the baby, but they witnessed the signing of the document.

Each entry begins with a section about the person who is appearing to record the birth, who in many cases is the father. If so, the information about him will appear at the beginning of the document, and in the place where the parents appear the father will simply be referred to as the *informante* or *declarante*. The same procedure is followed for marriages and deaths. Just one birth entry from a civil register can be extremely helpful in giving you information about your family lines.

## Parish Registers

It goes almost without saying that your Mexican ancestors were probably Catholic. The Catholic Church and the Catholic priest were an integral part of their daily lives. Whether they lived in a large city or a tiny village, whenever there was a birth, marriage, or death in the family, the priest was there to administer the appropriate sacrament of baptism, marriage vows, or last rites. Each of these events was then recorded in the sacramental books. For this reason, the parish registers will prove valuable to you in tracing your Mexican family history. This is likely to be true even if your ancestors were Jewish. Many Mexicans of Jewish descent converted to Catholicism.

Fortunately, 99 percent of the pre-1900 parish registers in Mexico have been microfilmed and are available through your Family History Center. To order these microfilms (as well as microfilms of the civil registers), look first in the Locality Section of the FHLC under your ancestor's town. One of the topics for the town will be Church Records, under which will be an inventory of the records that are microfilmed and the years they cover. After determining the film numbers for the years you need, fill out an order form requesting that film or films.

AUTHOR
Iglesia Católica. San Miguel (Cualac).

TITLE
Registros parroquiales, 1696–1965.

PUBLICATION INFORMATION
Salt Lake City: Filmado por la Sociedad Genealógica de Utah, 1969.

FORMAT
39 rollos; 35 mm.

NOTES
Microfilm de manuscritos en Cualac.

CONTENTS

| | LATIN AMERICA FILM AREA |
|---|---|
| Bautismos 1689–1822 | 0697831 item 1 |
| Bautismos 1696–1755 | 0694519 |
| Bautismos 1755–1804, 1817–1833 | 0694520 |
| Bautismos 1825–1850, 1853–1868 | 0694521 |
| Bautismos 1861–1877 | 0694522 |
| Bautismos 1868–1889 | 0694523 |
| Bautismos 1882–1899 | 0694524 |
| Bautismos 1899–1934 | 0694525 |
| Bautismos 1916–1947 | 0694526 |
| Bautismos 1936–1965 | 0694527 |
| Confirmaciones 1886–1906, 1910–1933, 1938–1948, 1959–1966 | 0694528 |
| Matrimonios 1697–1713, 1724–1739 | 0694529 |
| Matrimonios 1701–1702 | 0697831 item 2 |
| Matrimonios 1741–1773 | 0694530 |
| Matrimonios 1767–1791, 1826–1850, 1864–1885 | 0694531 |
| Matrimonios 1885–1913 | 0694532 |
| Matrimonios 1913–1965 | 0694533 |
| Defunciones 1696–1764 | 0694534 |
| Defunciones 1754–1771, 1833–1892, 1902–1956 | 0694535 |
| Información matrimonial 1783–1830 | 0694536 |
| Información matrimonial 1830 | 0694537 |
| Información matrimonial 1837–1846 | 0694538 |
| Información matrimonial 1846–1849 | 0694539 |
| Información matrimonial 1850–1864 | 0694540 |
| Información matrimonial 1864–1869 | 0694541 |
| Información matrimonial 1870–1872 | 0694542 |
| Información matrimonial 1872–1879 | 0694477 |
| Información matrimonial 1880–1887 | 0694478 |
| Información matrimonial 1887–1889 | 0694479 |
| Información matrimonial 1890–1892 | 0694480 |
| Información matrimonial 1892–1897 | 0694481 |

THIS RECORD FOUND UNDER
1. Mexico, Guerrero, Cualac—Church records

Now, let's suppose that in your home search you find a marriage record for your grandfather Alonso González Díaz in 1880, stating that he was born in the town of Cualac, Mexico. His parents are Francisco González Cruz and María Díaz Lozano. First you would find the town of Cualac, which is in the state of Guerrero, Mexico, in the FHLC. Page 118 shows that page of the FHLC. You then order the microfilms of baptisms and marriages for Cualac for the years 1840–1870 (film numbers 0694521, 0694522, and 0694531) through the Family History Center. Once received, you thread the film for baptisms covering the years 1825–1868 (film number 0694521) onto the microfilm reader.

The actual process of using microfilmed records is really quite easy. Probably the best way to start is to inventory the entire microfilm, going from one item number to the next and writing down the dates and type of records (births, marriages, deaths, or a combination of all three) that each item contains. Save this inventory in your permanent records. You will undoubtedly find yourself referring to it again and again as you find new information about the family and want to review certain time periods.

Now, let's suppose you want to find the birth date of your grandfather, Alonso González Díaz. You know that he was married in 1880. Supposing that he was married at about the age of twenty, you search the birth records starting in the year 1862 (which would have made him eighteen), looking for any children born to the couple Francisco González Cruz and María Díaz Lozano. Beginning with 1862, move back through the years 1861, 1860, 1859, and so on. You may not find his birth record for several years, but you will find one or two of his siblings (brothers or sisters). Record all the information for the births of the siblings as you would for your direct-line ancestor. Sometimes information is given for the birth of one child that may not be entered in the birth entry for another, such as the name of the town where one of the grandparents came from.

Using an abstract form to record your information is

incredibly helpful in making sure that you have all the information possible from each parish entry. A printed form also helps you track all the information available as you read through an entry. These forms are designed to be used either for civil registers or parish registers, so there will be spaces for more information than any one entry will contain.

Let's suppose it turns out your grandfather was twenty-five when he married, which means he was born in 1855. Once you have found his birth entry, continue looking for any other siblings until you have a period of at least ten to fifteen years with no more births for that couple. Then return to the date at which you started your search, 1862, and move the other way in time (1863, 1864, 1865, and so on), looking for any younger children. Continue until you have gone for a period of at least ten years with no further births.

You will, of course, want to be aware of any other families you could find during the time period you are searching. For example, if both your grandfather and your grandmother are from the same town, you may find your grandmother's birth or the birth of one of her siblings before you find any births for your grandfather's family. Because your grandparents' marriage certificate will list both sets of parents, you will know the names of both couples who could be parents.

## Indexes

Occasionally you will be lucky and find that the parish registers were indexed. Most indexes are done by first name rather than last name. For example, your grandfather Alonso would be listed under the A's. It didn't matter whether the baby was a boy or a girl; all the babies whose names started with the same letter would be indexed together. Indexes can be a wonderful help, but occasionally the compilers made mistakes. It's a good idea to go through the records page by page even if you cannot find the information you are looking for. A page-by-page search of the records shows you the same names spelled several different times, and the spelling may be clearer in one record than it is in another.

# Reading the Handwriting

Some of you may be saying by now, "Wait a minute! I can't even *read* these records." Be assured that you are not the first researcher to have these feelings. It can be done. In fact, with just a little patience and practice you will be amazed at what you can do.

You need to have at least some familiarity with Spanish. Enthusiasm can go a long way, but you will do better if you have had at least a few semesters of Spanish, or have spoken it a little at home.

Parish records are excellent for learning to do research because so much in them is consistent from document to document. Dates in parish entries are nearly always written out, such as "On the twenty-third day of September in the year of our Lord one thousand eight hundred and sixty three." The month and year will be written out in each entry unless words such as *de los mismos* or *del dicho mes y año* ("of the same" or "of the said month and year") are used.

Another repetition comes in the phrases that the priest used. Nearly always the wording in a baptismal entry will read *bautisé solemnamente a un niño* . . . ("I solemnly baptized a male child"), followed by the name of the child. A common phrasing in a marriage entry is *en facie eclesia* ("in front of the church"), followed by the name of the groom. Knowing these "clue phrases" can save you much time.

When you first look at an original document or a new roll of microfilm, take a few minutes to study the priest's handwriting. Begin with the parts of the document we have just discussed that remain consistent from entry to entry. The way the priest writes the date, his name, and key phrases will be clues. When you find a difficult letter, look for it in other parts of the document. One researcher had trouble reading a person's first name. When she reread the date she realized that the same capital "F" in the word *Febrero* was repeated in the name, which turned out to be Francisco.

Don't be surprised at variety or inconsistency, even within the same document. It is not uncommon to find the same word spelled different ways, or capitalized one time and lower-case another. When you have difficulty with any word, say it out loud. You will be surprised how often the meaning will become clear to you.

One excellent source is the manual called *Spanish Records Extraction*, written by researchers at The Church of Jesus Christ of Latter-day Saints specifically for volunteer workers who were extracting information from Spanish-language records. The workbook pages of this manual contain excellent examples along with short quizzes and answers to help you through the process of reading old Spanish handwriting.

## Writing Letters

Many family historians have had great success in getting documents from Mexico simply by writing letters. If you are unsure of your ability to write an entire letter in Spanish, ask a family member or a friend who speaks Spanish fluently to help you. You could also ask a Spanish teacher at either a local university or high school.

Your letter should begin with a request that is short and specific. Ask for only one or two names or certificates at a time. Write again if necessary.

Always ask for a copy of the document you are requesting. If you ask only for names and dates, the person responding will probably send just that, and you will miss the chance of finding any other details the document may contain.

At the conclusion of your letter, thank the person in advance for the time he or she has taken on your behalf. You will also have a better chance of being answered if money is included. Send enough to cover the person's time, any materials that are needed, and return postage. In this way you show your appreciation as well as your recognition of the value of the person's time.

If possible, type the letter. Be sure to include your return address in the body of your letter as well as on your envelope.

# SAMPLE LETTER REQUESTING RECORDS

Ajo, Arizona
15 de mayo 1996

Director
Registro Civil
Los Mochis, Sinaloa
Mexico

Estimado Señor Director:

Estoy preparando una historia de mi familia para la cual necesito copias de las siguientes partidas:

1. Partida de defunción de mi bisabuela Maria Melchora Sanchez quien murió en Los Mochis en el año 1938.
2. Partida de nacimiento de mi bisabuelo Juan Lopez, hijo de Jose Maria Lopez y Manuela Botello, quien nació en Los Mochis en el año 1898.
3. Partida de matrimonio de mis bisabuelos Maria Melchora Sanchez y Juan Lopez, hijo de Jose Maria Lopez y Manuela Botello, quienes se casaron en Los Mochis en el año 1923.

Incluyo con esta carta cinco dólares para los costos de copias literales. Si no es suficiente, indíqueme la cantidad adicional que debo enviarle para las copias literales de esos certificados.

Con anticipación de su amable servicio, le doy las gracias.

Su servidor,

David J. Lopez
211 First Street
Ajo, Arizona

# Resources

## RESEARCHING MEXICAN RECORDS

**Alvarez, José Rogelio.** *Enciclopedia de México.* **Mexico City: Secretaria de Educación Publica, 1987.**

This is the first volume of a multivolume series about the states of Mexico and their *municipios*. (Text in Spanish.)

**American Geographical Society.** *Index to the Map of Hispanic America.* **Washington, DC: American Geographical Society, 1945.**

This is an index to a series of detailed maps of all of Latin America.

**Aparicio, Edgar Juan. "Genealogical Research in Mexico and Central America, Part II: Central America," in** *World Conference on Records and Genealogical Seminar.* **Salt Lake City: The Genealogical Society of the Church of Jesus Christ of Latter-day Saints, 1969.**

This is a good summary of research in Mexico.

**Barton, Noel R. "Genealogical Research in the Records of the California Spanish Missions."** *Genealogical Journal* **4 (March 1975): 13–33.**

This good description of research in mission records includes a table of the record locations.

**Brown, Angel Sepulveda, and Cadena, Gloria V.** *San Agustin Parish of Laredo, Marriage Book II, 1858–1881.* **San Antonio: Los Bejareños, 1993.**

This is representative of the excellent computerizing and

indexing of parish records that is being done in the Southwest. If you are researching there, contact one of the societies listed in chapter 7 to see what other books like this one are available.

**Chipman, Donald E.** *Archives of the Archdiocese of Santa Fe, 1678–1900.* **Publications of the Academy of the American Franciscan History, Bibliographical Series, Vol. 3. Washington, DC: Academy of American Franciscan History, 1957.**

For New Mexican research, the Catholic Church archives this book describes are essential.

**Church of Jesus Christ of Latter-day Saints.** *Fuentes Principales de Registros Genealógicos en México.* **Series H, No. 2, Edición Español. Salt Lake City: La Sociedad Genealógica de La Iglesia de Jesucristo de los Santos de los Ultimos Dias, 1970.**

This Spanish-language pamphlet summarizing Mexican records, also available in English, is a good place to start to look beyond parish records. (Text in Spanish.)

———. *Spanish Handwriting.* **Series H, No. 22. Salt Lake City: The Genealogical Department of the Church of Jesus Christ of Latter-day Saints, 1979.**

This pamphlet on how to read old handwritten records contains excellent alphabet charts.

———. *Spanish Records Extraction.* **Salt Lake City: The Church of Jesus Christ of Latter-day Saints, 1981.**

The workbook format of this book makes it an excellent training manual for learning to read the handwriting in old parish records.

**Cottler, Susan M.** *Finding Aids to the Microfilmed Manuscript Collection of the Genealogical Society of Utah: Preliminary Survey of the Mexican Collection.* **Salt Lake City: University of Utah Press, 1978.**

A survey of all of the Mexican Catholic Church parish records and civil registers filmed by the Mormon Church. Additional ones have been filmed since 1978. Check the FHLC for an updated list.

**Guide to Film 811: Parish Archives of Sonora and Sinaloa. Tucson: Microforms Section, University of Arizona Library, 1976.**

This guide will lead you to Sonoran and Sinaloan parish records not filmed by the Mormons.

**Lo Buglio, Rudecinda. "The Archives of Northwestern Mexico," in Latin American and Iberian Family and Local History, Vol. 9, World Conference on Records. Salt Lake City: Genealogical Society of Utah, 1980.**

This article identifies archives, especially parish archives, in northwestern Mexico, including some not filmed by the Mormons.

**———. "Baja California Mission Records" and "La Familia de Arce de Baja California." Antepasados II. San Francisco: Los Californianos, 1977.**

The first article reviews the sacramental records of the Baja California missions. The second is an example of a good family history. (Text of second article is in Spanish.)

**Martínez, Pablo L. Guia Familiar de Baja California, 1700–1900. Mexico City: Imprenta "Laura," 1965.**

This is an extensive compilation of most existing parish records in Baja California and also includes some biographies and oral interviews. (Text in Spanish.)

**Martínez, Thomas. Santa Cruz de la Cañada Baptisms, 1710 to 1854. San Jose, CA: Thomas Martínez, 1992.**

This is another example of the computerizing and indexing of parish records in the United States.

**McDonald, Dendra S. Guide to the Spanish and Mexi-**

*can Manuscript Collection at the Catholic Archives of Texas.* Edited by Kinga Perzynska. Austin: Catholic Archives of Texas, 1994.

> For those researching in Texas, this is a guide to an essential archival collection, including many early parish records not yet microfilmed.

O'Gorman, Edmundo. *Historia de las Divisiones Territoriales de Mexico*, 4th ed. "Sepan Cuantos," no. 45. Mexico City: Editorial Porrúa, S.A., 1968.

> This is a history of the many changes in the political divisions in Mexico. It may be useful for tracking down records in a region that has changed names. (Text in Spanish.)

Platt, Lyman D. *Genealogical Research in Latin America and the Hispanic United States.* St. George, UT: Teguayo Press, 1993.

> A good overview of Hispanic genealogical research. The discussion of the origin and frequency of the most common Hispanic surnames is particularly interesting.

———. *México, Guía General: Divisiones Eclesiásticas.* Salt Lake City: Instituto Genealógico e Histórico Latinoamericano, 1989.

> This book is a "must buy" for anyone doing serious research in Mexico; it identifies the dioceses and parishes of Mexico, when they started, and where to find the parish records. (Text in Spanish.)

———. *México, Guía General: Divisiones Políticas.* Salt Lake City: Instituto Genealógico e Histórico Latinoamericano, 1989.

> This book describes the municipal and other civil government units where you would look for civil registers and other governmental records. (Text in Spanish.)

Radding, Cynthia de Murrieta, and Torres, María

**Lourdes Chávez.** *Catálogo del Archivo de la Parroquia de la Purísima Concepción de los Alamos, 1685–1900, Catálogo 22.* **Hermosillo, Mexico: Centro Regional del Noroeste, 1976.**

> This detailed description of the parish records of Alamos, Mexico, is representative of the catalogs that exist for some parishes in Mexico. (Text in Spanish.)

**Robinson, David J.** *Finding Aids to the Microfilmed Manuscript Collection of the Genealogical Society of Utah: Research Inventory of the Mexican Collection of Colonial Parish Records.* **Salt Lake City: University of Utah Press, 1980.**

> A survey of all of the colonial era Mexican Catholic Church records filmed by the Mormon Church. Additional records have been filmed since 1978; check the FHLC if the record you need is not listed here.

## MODERN ATLASES AND MAPS

Individual atlases that exist for most Hispanic countries can help locate ancestral towns and establish the proximity of ancestral towns to other towns found during research. Typical of these atlases is one for Mexico, *Nuevo Atlas Porrúa de la República Mexicana* (Mexico, D.F.: Editorial Porrúa, 1980), available in many local libraries. This small volume contains maps of each state, historical maps, and a general countrywide index, as well as various geographical entity lists.

Another useful geographical tool for the Latin American genealogist is the *Index to the Map of Hispanic America*, published by the American Geographical Society (Washington, DC: 1945). As this is an index to a collection of maps, scale 1:1,000,000, it will generally be found only in a large public or university library. It covers all Latin American countries in good detail.

Also of value for locating especially small hamlets and for recreating geographical details of local life are the *United*

*States Army Map Service Select Series* and *Topographical Maps* produced for all of these countries. Any place, no matter how small, will appear on these detailed maps (scale 1:50,000). Unfortunately, the maps have no direct index, and locating places can only be accomplished by using latitude and longitude references in the gazetteers such as those published by the U.S. Office of Geography. (See the following section on gazetteers.)

Maps and atlases are being digitalized for computer storage at a rapid rate. As that process continues, these will become increasingly available on CD-ROM and on the Internet and World Wide Web. Currently, for example, the University of Texas at Austin Perry Castañeda Library Map Collection has placed many atlases and maps from the CIA on the Internet. Check with the library for the current address and the countries available.

**Atlas de los estados de la república Mexicana y planos urbanos de las principales ciudades. Mexico, D.F.: HFET, S.A. de C.V., 1993. (BYU Maps G 1545 .H33× 1993)**

(Text in Spanish.)

**Collecion Enciclopedia de los municipios de México. Mexico, D.F.: Secretaria de Gobernacion, 1988.**

(Text in Spanish.)

**García de Mirarda, Enriqueta, and Falcón de Gyves, Zaida. Nuevo atlas Porrúa de la república mexicana. Mexico, D.F.: Editorial Porrúa, 1989. (FHL)**

(Text in Spanish.)

## GAZETTEERS

Gazetteers are lists of place names with a minimal amount of information to identify and locate each particular place. Since many gazetteers list geographical subdivisions smaller than the parish or municipality, and other features such as rivers and mountains, they can be of great help when the particular place to be located does not appear in the atlases or geographical dictionaries available to the researcher. Many countries also publish postal guides and political division guides.

Gazetteers, such as the *United States Board on Geographical Names Gazetteer,* prepared by the Office of Geography of the Department of the Interior, are frequently more readily obtained in the United States than local geographical dictionaries and detailed atlases of Hispanic countries. The one for Mexico is number 15. There is also an updated version of these gazetteers published by the Defense Mapping Agency (DMA). This gazetteer has now been placed by the DMA (in collaboration with the U.S. Board of Geographic Names) on the Internet under the title GEOnet Names Server.

**Division municipal de las entidades federativas. Mexico, D.F.: Dirección General de Estadística, 1938. (FHL film 1102985 item 1–4, 0896970 item 3)**

(Text in Spanish.)

**Gazetteer of Mexico, Vols. I and II, 3d ed. Washington, DC: Defense Mapping Agency, 1992. (BYU F 1204 .G38 1992 3 Vols.)**

**Hinton, Rose Marie B. Places of México. Salt Lake City: Instituto Genealógico e Histórico Latinoamericano, 1987. (FHL)**

**Localidades de la República por entidades federativas y municipios (del) VIII censo general de población, 1960. Mexico, D.F.: Talleres Gráficos de la Nación, 1963. (FHL film 0873575)**

(Text in Spanish.)

**Peñafiel, Antonio. División municipal de la república**

*mexicana.* Mexico, D.F.: Ministerio de Fomento, 1896. (FHL 0896837 item 4)

(Text in Spanish.)

## GEOGRAPHICAL DICTIONARIES

These vary in size, from one- and two-volume dictionaries to large series containing sixteen to twenty volumes. In the United States, those covering Mexico are found in the *Family History Library Catalog* or in large public or university libraries that have map collections. Mexico also has state or regional geographic dictionaries. Whether national or regional, these are most helpful in locating a particular town and usually provide a written description of the town or other geographical unit. These descriptions, as well as individual place-name entries, can be used to identify the larger geographical unit (where records would usually be found) to which a smaller unit, whose name is the only one the family remembers, belongs. These dictionaries also often provide information if you want to develop the history of the ancestral locality as a background to the family history.

*Diccionario Porrúa de história, biografía y geografía de México.* Mexico, D.F.: Editorial Porrúa, 1976. (BYU F 1204 .D56 1976 2 Vols.)

(Text in Spanish.)

*Diccionario universal de história y de geografía.* Vol. 1–4. Mexico, D.F.: Tipografía de Rafael, 1853. (FHL film Vol. 1–2 0599332, Vol. 3 1162477 item 10, Vol. 4 0599333)

(Text in Spanish.)

Garcia Cubas, Antonio. *Diccionario geográfico, histórico y biográfico de los estados unidos Méxicanos.* Mexico, D.F.: Antigua Impr. de Murguia,

1888–91. (BYU F 1204 .G2 5 Vols.) (FHL film 1102587 Vol. 1–3, 1102588 Vol. 4–5)

(Text in Spanish.)

## HISTORICAL ATLASES, MAPS, AND MATERIALS

These are geographic reference tools that were printed before 1900 but are still widely available or were written to deal with geography during a historical period, most often the colonial period.

**Burrus, Ernest J.** *La obra cartográfica de la provincia Mexicana de la Compañía de Jesús (1567–1967).* **Madrid: José Porrúa Turanzas, 1967. (FHL)**

(Text in Spanish.)

**Day, James M.; Dunlap, Ann B.; Smyers, Mike; and Parker, Kenneth.** *Maps of Texas, 1527–1990: The Map Collection of the Texas State Archives.* **Austin: Pemberton Press, 1964.**

Maps are important to successful research. This book will guide you to those of Texas.

**Gerhard, Peter.** *Geografía histórica de la Nueva España, 1519–1821.* **Mexico City: Universidad Nacional Autónoma de México, 1986.**

(Text in Spanish.)

————. *The North Frontier of New Spain.* **Norman: University of Oklahoma Press, 1982. (BYU F 1229 .G47)**

————. *The Southeast Frontier of New Spain.* **Norman: University of Oklahoma Press, 1993. (BYU F 1231 .G42 1993)**

*A Guide to the Historical Geography of New Spain.*

Cambridge, UK: Cambridge University Press, 1972. (FHL)

## ECCLESIASTICAL DIRECTORIES

Many Catholic dioceses publish directories listing the various parishes, seminaries, and convents that make up the diocese. These directories always include the names of local parishes and the priests who serve there. They also may contain maps and other aids, and interesting and pertinent information about local history, including local jurisdictional changes. Many of these directories are available through the LDS Family History Centers and in libraries having the CIDOC Collection of Latin American Church documents on microfilm.

*Directorio de la Iglesia en México.* Mexico City: Buena Prensa, 1952. (CIDOC Collection No. 21014)

(Text in Spanish.)

*Directorio eclesiástico.* México: Arzobispado de México, 1968. (FHL)

(Text in Spanish.)

Mendoza, P. Alfredo Galindo. *Apuntes geográficos y estadísticos de la Iglesia Católica en México.* Mexico City: Administraction de la Revista "La Cruz," 1945. (FHL, CIDOC Collection no. 21076)

(Text in Spanish.)

Platt, Lyman D. *Mexico: guía general: divisiones eclesiásticas.* Salt Lake City: Instituto Genealógico e Histórico Latinoamericano, 1989. (FHL)

(Text in Spanish.)

Romero Ortigozo, José Antonio. *Directorio de la iglesia en México.* Mexico City: Buena Prensa, 1952. (FHL film 1224501 item 3)

(Text in Spanish.)

# Chapter 6

# Other Documents: Making Your Ancestors Come Alive

Family history research becomes much more exciting if we can go beyond the basic facts about our ancestors. Two of the most useful and valuable types of documents for helping us get to know our Mexican ancestors are census records and notarial records. The information contained in these documents can give us an actual glimpse into the lives of our ancestors, and perhaps the neighborhoods and homes where they lived.

## Census Records

A census record is a count of all the people in a city or rural district. Think for a minute of the work involved in taking a census, especially in frontier areas before modern forms of transportation. A census taker would go to every house in a city or town, and at each house he would take a count of all the people who lived there. In addition to their names, he would ask them other information that the government required him to obtain. He would enter all this information on a special form and return the form to his supervisor, who would store it in a central government building.

The government kept the records to get a count of the people for taxes and for military service. But today as we read the information the census taker recorded, we can appreciate the details that a census contains.

Because the census taker went from house to house, his record ended up documenting the neighborhood as well as each family. Even a single page from a census contains the names of several families. You begin to get a feeling for the community.

A census was usually divided into columns with the following categories of information. We will demonstrate how to obtain information from a census by examining a page from the 1930 census for the city of Cañones in the state of Sonora.

*Nombre/Apellido* (Name/Surname)—A census never tells you for certain all the members of each family. Instead, you need to make deductions based upon last names and ages. Remember the Hispanic surname system as it relates to women. The woman keeps the surnames she was born with throughout her life, even after she is married. This would help you to understand the entries for the individuals in the Cañones census numbered 4, 5, 6, and 7. Number 4 is a male, age twenty-nine, named Francisco de P. Monteverde. (This is the same as the census taker's name in the upper lefthand corner. Do you think they are the same person?) Number 5 is a female, age twenty-five, named Francisca Ballestero. Numbers 6 and 7 are two children, ages three and one, named Fidelino Monteverde and Martí Omar Monteverde. Based on this information, we could make the tentative assumption that numbers 4 and 5, Francisco Monteverde and Francisca Ballestero, are married to each other and numbers 6 and 7 (who have the same last name as their father) are their children. The mother would still be using the last name she has used since her birth, Ballestero.

*Sexo* (Sex)—This column is divided into two categories, male and female. The census taker has put a "+" sign in the appropriate box for each person.

*Edad* (Age)—Beneath this heading are the three categories of years, months, and days. The census taker has written each person's age in the box corresponding to his or her name. For babies less than a year old he has written the number of months of their age.

*Estado Civil* (Marital Status)—This box refers to the person's "civil state," or in other words, their marital status. Beneath this heading are six categories: Single; Married

Civilly; Married by the Church; Free Union (living together without being married); Widow(er); Divorced. It is interesting that numbers 4 and 5, 11 and 12, and 27 and 28 were married both civilly and in the church. Numbers 25 and 26 lived together without being married.

*Profesion o Ocupacion* (Profession or Occupation)—A glance at the occupations listed in a census will give you a feeling for what the area was like. Number 4, Francisco Monteverde, is a *mecanico*. His neighbor on one side is a cobbler (a person who makes and repairs shoes), and the one on the other side is a miner. It is also interesting that the eleven- and twelve-year-old children listed are identified as "scholars," meaning that they went to school. The fact that this was noted makes us wonder if other children of this age were not so fortunate. Many of the men in the Cañones census were miners. What does it tell us about the area around Cañones?

*Lugar de Nacimiento* (Place of Birth)—This is an especially helpful category for researchers who do not yet know the birthplace of their ancestor. Finding the birthplace of family members can lead you to other documents in parish and state (civil) records for that locality. It is fascinating that in this "neighborhood" in Cañones there is one person from China. What do you think led him from China to Mexico?

*Idioma* (Language Spoken)—The first column under this category asks if the person speaks Castilian (Spanish). Everyone does except for the young children. The next column asks if another language or dialect is spoken. The person born in China speaks Chinese, and there are three on the page who speak English.

*Bienes Raices* (Real Property Owned)—Only five of the ten families owned property. What would this indicate about the distribution of wealth in the community?

*Defectos Fisicos o Mentales* (Physical or Mental Defects)— Nobody on this page has a physical or mental defect.

*Religion* (Religion)—As you would expect in a Hispanic nation, the majority of these people are Catholics. The Chinese man is listed as having no religion.

*Sin Trabajar* (Without Work)—This column tells how long a person has been out of work. Three men were in this situation at the time the census was taken, including number 4, Francisco Monteverde, who has been out of work as a mechanic for sixty days. Do you think this might be the reason he is also working as a census taker?

As you can see, a census record listing one of your ancestral families can be a valuable find. With a little study and imagination, you will be able to piece together new information and understanding about your family members and the locality in which they lived.

During the eighteenth and nineteenth centuries censuses gave less information. Many, however, even in the 1700s, often contain good information. Let's look at a census for the area of Saltillo, Mexico, in 1777. The first family the census taker found there is described as follows:

> Don José Sartuche, Spaniard, citizen and worker, his age forty-three years, married to María Theresa del Bosque, Spaniard, thirty years old. They have eight children. They are: three single males: Juan José eleven years, José Joachin seven years, José Simón one month, María Antonia fifteen years, Juana thirteen years, Leonarda eleven years, Susa nine years, Francisca four years, one servant Alexandro Calidos, Indian, native of the valley and a worker, his profession shepherd, age thirty-five years married to María Ramirez, free mulatta, thirty-two years old. They have three children: José seven years, Juana five years, María three years. Another servant, Spaniard citizen and worker, single, twenty-five years old.

Each of the families on the page is headed by a man whose last name is Sartuche, whose ages are forty-three, forty, thirty, and twenty-five. Do you think they might all be brothers?

Where can one find census records? Once again, begin your search in the local Family History Center of the Mormon Church. Look first in the Family History Library Catalog under your ancestor's locality. Look under both the name of the city by itself and the name of the city as a municipality (*municipio*). If you don't find census records there, look up your town in the book *Latin American Census Records* by Lyman Platt, listed in the **Resources**.

## Notarial Records

Another person who can help you in doing family history research is the notary. In Spain and Latin America the notary did what many attorneys do today in the United States. When somebody needed a will, or sold a piece of land, or made a prenuptial agreement (a contract stating what the bride and groom each bring to the marriage), a notary drew up the document for them. However, notaries went beyond the scope of American attorneys by witnessing the signing of these documents and filing all the documents they drafted each year in a book called a *protocolo*. These *protocolos* became the official records of notarial transactions.

Let's look at what is found in a will. In Spanish the word for a "will" is *testamento*. In English we call the person who makes a will a "testator." Testators made wills in order to leave instructions as to what they wanted done following their deaths. Specific directions were given for the procedure to be followed regarding their burial, and what they wanted done with their property.

After the words *En el nombre de Dios, Amen* ("In the name of God, Amen"), the next sentences in a will give the name of the person whose will it is. If he or she is married, it gives the name of the spouse and whether or not the spouse is deceased. If the person making the will never married, it gives the names of his or her parents. This helps you be certain that you have the will of the ancestor you are searching for, and it may give you the names of a new generation you did not know before.

Next, the testator states how he or she wants to be buried. In Mexico, as in all Hispanic countries, the people are predominantly Catholic. They leave instructions about masses they want said on their behalf, and also masses that they would like to have said for relatives who have already died. This might give you information about family members you did not know about. For example, a woman might have masses said for children who have already died.

This part of the will also gives directions as to where the person wants to be buried. Today nearly everybody is buried in a cemetery. Depending on the time and place your ancestor died, however, he or she may have been buried in the church. It was common practice in many places to bury the dead under the floor of the chapel in the church. The floor was laid with large stones, and one of the stones would be lifted and the body lowered into that spot. Typical requests you might find are of people wanting to be buried "by my spouse, under the fourth stone from the altar."

Once the religious requests have been declared, the person making the will then specifies what should be done with his or her property. This is a fascinating part of the will for you as a family historian, because it gives you some indication as to the lifestyle of your ancestor. It is interesting that both men and women in Mexico owned property. In one study made of the wills of twelve women living in what is now New Mexico during the years 1715–1768, it was found that eleven of the twelve owned property.

Because most people had so little, everything a person owned was valuable. Wills dealt with property such as land and buildings, but also included small items such as a hoe, a spoon, or stockings. One will left "a pitcher used for chocolate." Many times articles of clothing were left to family members. One woman left her brown shawl to her daughter-in-law to thank her for the care she had given her. Many times stepchildren were mentioned. Family servants were also given property in some instances.

In nearly all cases, each living child of the testator is mentioned by name. Often this is in a part of the will listing the heirs who divide up the property not specifically given to someone. If the testator's child is deceased but has living children, the names of those grandchildren might be given.

All of these facts tell you who was alive in your ancestor's family at that point in time.

Even the closing of a will can tell you about your ancestor. Whether or not he or she is able to sign the will speaks to his or her educational level. None of the women in the New Mexico study signed their names.

## Where Can I Find Notarial Documents?

Many notarial documents, including wills, have been microfilmed. Once again you can find these in your Family History Center. Check the FHLC in a locality search under the name of the place and/or the capital city for the topics of notarial records or wills.

As discussed in the last chapter, parish death records may lead you to the will of an ancestor. Death records frequently state whether the deceased had made a will, and if so, who the notary was. Once you know the name of the notary, you can find the wills he notarized by doing an author search in the Family History Library Catalog. Use the ancestor's death date as a starting point for your search and move backward in time. In other words, if he died on June 16, 1899, start at that date in the notarial records and move to June 15, June 14, and so on.

If you are unable to find notarial records on microfilm, write to the Archivo Municipal or the Archivo Estatal in the town and/or state where your ancestor lived to ask if they have notarial records for the time and place in which you are searching.

## Other Records

Many other records are available in Mexico. Newspapers, Inquisition records, marriage dispensations, cemetery records, government activity reports, tax lists, and court records are among them. A thorough search of all the topics in the Family History Library Catalog under the name of your ancestral hometown will help you locate the sources available to you.

# Resources

## CENSUSES AND NOTARIAL DOCUMENTS

**Barnes, Thomas; Naylor, Thomas H; and Polzer, Charles W. *Northern New Spain: A Research Guide*. Tucson: University of Arizona Press, 1981.**

This introduction to the computerized index of Northern New Spain (pre-1821) describes notarial and other documents for the areas of colonial Mexico and the southwestern United States north of Durango, Mexico. Also found are lists of Indian tribes and local government and ecclesiastical units.

**Boyd-Bowman, Peter. *Indice y extractos del Archivo de Protocolos de Puebla de los Angeles, México (1538–1556)*. Madison, WI: Hispanic Seminary of Medieval Studies, 1988.**

Extracts of the earliest sixteenth-century notarial documents from the city of Puebla. (Text in Spanish.)

**Cavazos Garza, Israel. *Catálogo y síntesis de los protocolos del archivo municipal de Monterrey, 1599–1786*. 4 vols. Monterrey, Mexico: La Academia Mexicana de la Historia, 1966–1986.**

Extracts from the earliest notarial records from Monterrey, Mexico. (Text in Spanish.)

**Espinosa, J. Manuel. "Population of the El Paso District in 1692." *Mid-America, A Historical Quarterly*, Vol. 23. Institute of Jesuit History, Loyola University, Chicago (1941).**

This is the 1692 census of El Paso, Texas.

**Kielman, Chester V.** *Guide to the Microfilm Edition of the Bexar Archives, 1717–1803.* Austin: University of Texas Archives, 1967.

The Bexar archives contain notarial records and censuses for the Spanish colonial period in Texas.

**Lo Buglio, Rudecinda Ann, FAS.** **"La Villa de Sinaloa Año de 1748: Two Military Lists."** *Spanish-American Genealogist* **(Annual 1979).**

This is a published 1748 military census for the town of Sinaloa, Mexico.

**Mantecon, J. I., and Carlo, A. Millares.** *Indice y extractos de los Protocolos del Archivo de Notarías de México, D.F. (I. 1524–1528, II. 1536–1538 and 1551–1553).* 2 vols. Mexico City: El Colegio de México, 1945.

These extracts of the earliest sixteenth-century notarial documents from Mexico City begin only four years after Cortés conquered the Aztec capital. (Text in Spanish.)

**Northrop, Marie E. "The Los Angeles Padron of 1844."** *Historical Society of Southern California Quarterly* **42 (December 1960).**

This is a published census for the town of Los Angeles at the end of Mexican rule in California.

**Olmsted, Virginia L.** *New Mexico Spanish and Mexican Colonial Censuses, 1790, 1823, 1945.* Albuquerque: New Mexico Genealogical Society, 1975.

**———, comp.** *Spanish and Mexican Censuses of New Mexico, 1750 to 1830.* Albuquerque: New Mexico Genealogical Society, 1981.

These are collections of fully transcribed and translated colonial censuses for New Mexico with indexes.

**Pérez Fernández del Castillo, Bernardo.** *Historia de la escribanía en la Nueva España y del notariado en*

*México*. Mexico, D.F.: Colegio de Notarios del Distrito Federal and Editorial Porrúa, 1994.

This history of the notarial system in Mexico since the colonial period shows how notaries documented the full panorama of life. (Text in Spanish.)

Platt, Lyman D. *Latin American Census Records*, 2d ed. Salt Lake City: Instituto Genealógico Histórico Latinoamericano, 1992.

This book lists censuses for specific places in Mexico and the colonial southwestern United States.

*Residents of Texas, 1782–1836*. 3 vols. Austin: The University of Texas Institute of Texan Cultures, 1984.

These volumes are a transcription and translation of nearly all of the Spanish censuses of Texas.

Rock, Rosalind Z. "Mujeres de Sustancia: Women of Property in Northern New Spain." *Colonial Latin American Historical Review* (Fall 1993): 425–440.

This article looks at the lives of women in northern Mexico during the colonial era through the wills they left.

Timmons, W. H. "The Population of the El Paso Area—A Census of 1784." *New Mexico Historical Review* 52 (Oct. 1977): 311–16.

This census of El Paso, Texas, is annotated with biographical and family data.

Veyna, Angelina F. "'It Is My Last Wish That . . .': A Look at Colonial Nuevo Mexicanas Through Their Testaments," in *Building With Our Hands: New Directions in Chicana Studies*. Edited by Adela de la Torre and Beatriz M. Pesquera. Berkeley: University of California Press, 1993.

This article shows what life was like for colonial New Mexican women and demonstrates the fascinating information that can be gleaned from wills.

# Chapter 7
# Where Do I Go from Here?

## Mexican Archives

Most of the research we have discussed in this book, and probably most of the research you have done so far, has been limited to civil registers, parish registers, national censuses, and perhaps notarial records. Beyond this, however, an enormous variety of record types are available to the Mexican American researcher.

Archives are places where original records are stored. In Mexico, archives are maintained by government units as well as by the Catholic Church. Documents about city governments are stored in municipal archives, and records for the state are stored in state archives. Records for the entire country are stored in the national archives, the Archivo General de la Nación, which is housed in an old prison called Lecumberi in Mexico City. (Some government units, however, have not transferred their records to the Mexican National Archives. For example, naval and army records are found in separate archives controlled by the services.) Records for local Catholic Church units are housed in parish archives.

Some records of interest to Mexican Americans are also held in the four principal national archives in Spain (in the cities of Valladolid, Madrid, Barcelona, and Seville). The **Resources** at the end of this chapter list several guides to the collections of Spanish archives.

Don't be afraid to explore the possibilities of record types that can be found in all of these archives. Many of the records have been filmed. A thorough investigation of the FHLC will show you what is available for your ancestor's locality. Check also in the catalogs listed in the **Resources**

If your family has been part of a Christian congregation, church records and parish records in both the United States and Mexico can be valuable sources of genealogical information. Above, Father Restituto Pérez stands before the altar built in honor of Our Lady of Guadalupe, the patron saint of Mexico, at St. Pius Catholic Church in Chicago.

at the end of this chapter for universities in California, Arizona, New Mexico, and Texas that also have microfilmed records.

Following are some examples of Mexican American family history resources available in Mexican archives:

> *Marriage Dispensation Records.* Anybody marrying in the Catholic Church who was related in the fourth degree of consanguinity (meaning there was a common great-great-grandparent) needed to have a dispensation from the bishop. Because these documents were drawn up by the bishop (or one of his representatives) rather than the priest, they are stored in diocesan archives. A marriage dispensation could be anywhere from one or two pages to several pages long. In it, the person making the document would find out from townspeople how the couple who wanted to be married were related. In many cases the dispensation includes a family tree going back four generations to the common descendant.
>
> *Government Reports.* During the colonial period it was common practice for provincial governors and military commanders to submit long, detailed reports of daily life and events to the Viceroy in Mexico City and the Council of the Indies in Madrid. Many of the reports sent to the Viceroy in Mexico City are found today in collections called *ramos* in the Archivo General de la Nación. In the *ramo* called *provincias internas,* the government reports for northern Mexico and the southern United States can be found. The *ramo* called *Californias* contains reports of Baja California and Alta California. The University of Arizona at Tucson and the Bancroft Library at the University of California at Berkeley have copies of these collections.
>
> *Court Records.* These records contain a variety of judicial proceedings, generally found in state archives, although they may also be found on a municipal level. Among them are records of criminal prosecutions, lawsuits about contracts or land disputes, and for some time periods, divorce proceedings.

*Tax Lists.* You can find tax lists in archives at all government levels. In these documents you can find taxes assessed on such things as wine, wool, and cattle in addition to property. One Mexican community even assessed a tax to pay for the new piano teacher.

*Inquisition Records.* The Inquisition was handled by a branch of the Catholic Church charged with searching out heretics (those who didn't follow traditional Catholic belief), Protestants, and Jews. The records of their proceedings are found in the Archivo General de la Nación in Mexico City and are available through your local Family History Center in the FHLC.

*Ordinations to the Priesthood.* A careful record was kept of everybody who was ordained to the priesthood. Because these are records made by the Catholic bishop, they are kept in diocesan archives.

*Government Employee Records.* These records can be found in either state or national archives. If one of your ancestors or a sibling worked for the government, these records might give you added information about your family and their occupations.

*Cemetery Records.* City or municipal cemeteries began only after the colonial period. Before that time, burials took place in the church. Cemetery records are usually found in municipal archives.

*Land Records.* If your ancestors owned land, you might be able to find documents in notarial records concerning the sales of land and water rights, land ownership registrations, and land tax records. They can be found in archives at the municipal or state level, or even at the Archivo General de la Nación in Mexico City.

## Mexican American Research Groups

The increasing interest in Mexican American family history is evident in the growing number of organizations being formed specifically to help researchers. The names and addresses of several such groups are included in the **Resources**. If none of them are in your area, inquire at your

Family History Center or ask the librarian at your library.

You will undoubtedly find that these groups include people of varying research experience, from beginners to qualified experts. As you talk with them, you will find that their experiences can give you ideas and suggestions for your own research. Some groups have a common book or computer index where they enter the surnames they are searching and the areas where their ancestors are from. In this way those who are sharing the same research interests can network together.

If there is no research group in your area, be open to the possibility of forming one. Groups such as the Society for Hispanic Historical and Ancestral Research (SHHAR), based in southern California, will be glad to help you with the details involved in forming your own research unit.

Perhaps the best part of joining a research organization is the friendships you will make. Because they recognize the importance of families, people who do family history research tend to be warm and caring, full of enthusiasm and appreciation for life. When you attend a meeting of a thriving research group, you can sense a feeling of camaraderie among its members.

In chapter 1 we talked about the important role that you can play in society as a Mexican American. As you continue to be involved with Mexican American research, be aware of the possibility of becoming involved in genealogical organizations on a national level. Both the National Genealogical Society and the Federation of Genealogical Societies have annual conferences. They are sure to be advertised at your Family History Center and local library. If one is held near you, try to attend. As increasing numbers of Mexican American (and other Hispanic) researchers voice their research needs in a positive manner, more resources will become available to them on a local and national level.

# Resources

## GENEALOGICAL SOCIETIES

**Genealogical Society of Hispanic America**
P.O. Box K
Denver, CO 80209

**Genealogical Society of Hispanic America—Southern California Branch**
P.O. Box 2472
Santa Fe Springs, CA 90670
Periodical: *Huellas del Pasado*

**Hispanic Genealogical Society**
P.O. Box 1792
Houston, TX 77251-1792

**Los Bexareños Genealogical Society**
P.O. Box 1935
San Antonio, TX 78297
Periodical: *Los Bexareños Genealogical Register*

**Los Californianos**
4002 St. James Place
San Diego, CA 92103-1630

**Society for Hispanic Historical and Ancestral Research** (SHHAR)
P.O. Box 5294
Fullerton, CA 92635
Periodical: *Somos Primos*

Spanish American Genealogical Association
P.O. Box 5407
Corpus Christi, TX 78405

## INDEXES AND ARCHIVES

Archivo de Simancas. *Secretaria de Guerra, Hojas de Servicios de América*. Valladolid, Spain: Patronato Nacional de Archivos Históricos, 1958.

> Index of the service records found in the Simancas archives in Spain for Spanish soldiers serving in the American colonies. (Text in Spanish.)

Bancroft, Hubert H. *California Pioneer Register and Index, 1542–1848*. Baltimore: Genealogical Publishing Co., 1964.

> This collection of brief biographies of pre-1849 California pioneers includes many Mexicans.

Barredo de Valenzuela, Adolfo. *Indice de Insertos en XXV Años de la Revista "Hidalguía."* Madrid: Hidalguía, 1989.

> This index to the first twenty-five years of Spain's premier genealogical journal has many references to persons and places in Mexico. (Text in Spanish.)

Basanta de la Riva, Alfredo. *Sala de los Hijosdalgo*. Madrid: Instituto Internacional de Genealogía y Heráldica, 1955.

> This index to records of the Spanish nobility includes many references to people in Mexico. (Text in Spanish.)

Beers, Henry Putney. *Spanish and Mexican Records of the American Southwest*. Tucson: University of Arizona Press, 1979.

> This is an excellent study identifying the wealth of sources of records for the colonial Spanish period in the Southwest.

**Benavides, Adan, Jr.** *The Bexar Archives 1717–1836, A Name Guide.* **Austin: University of Texas Press for the University of Texas Institute of Texan Cultures at San Antonio, 1989.**

If your ancestors were in the area around San Antonio, Texas, during the colonial period, they should appear in this index.

**Bermudez Plata, Cristobal (vols. 1–3); Romera Iruela, Luis (vols. 4–5); and María del Carmen Galbis Diez (vols. 4–7).** *Catálogo de Pasajeros a Indias.* **Vol. 1: 1509–1534; Vol. 2: 1535–1538; Vol. 3: 1539–1559; Vol. 4: 1560–1566; Vol. 5 1567–1577; Vol. 6: 1578–1585; Vol. 7: 1586–1599. Seville: Imprenta Editorial de la Gavidia, 1940–1986.**

Check to see if any of your ancestors are included in this index of the official list of passengers sailing from Spain to the Americas. (Text in Spanish.)

**———.** *El Archivo General de Indias de Sevilla, sede del americanismo.* **Madrid: Cuerpo Facultativo de Archiveros, Bibliotecarios y Arquelogos, 1951.**

This book describes the General Archives of the Indies in Seville, Spain, which house huge collections covering the colonial era in the American colonies. (Text in Spanish.)

**Bolton, Herbert E.** *Guide to Materials for the History of the United States in the Principal Archives of Mexico.* **New York: Kraus Reprint Corp., 1985. (First printed in 1913.)**

This guide shows the wealth of records in Mexico dealing with the history of the American Southwest.

**Boyd-Bowman, Peter.** *Indice bio-geográfico de 40 mil pobladores españoles de América en el Siglo XVI.* **Bogota, Colombia: Instituto Cara y Cuervo, 1964.**

This author has searched many records to list thousands

of Spanish and Portuguese who came to New Spain and elsewhere in the Americas during the sixteenth century. (Text in Spanish.)

———. *Indice geo-biográfico de 56 mil pobladores de América*. Mexico, D.F.: Fondo de Cultura Económica, 1985.

(Text in Spanish.)

**Caballero, César; Delgado, Susana; and Newman, Bud.** *Mexico and the Southwest: Microfilm Holdings of Historical Documents and Rare Books at the University of Texas at El Paso Library*. **El Paso: University of Texas at El Paso Special Collections Department, 1984.**

This catalog identifies documents about Mexican history at the University of Texas at El Paso.

**Chapman, Charles E.** *Catalogue of Materials in the Archivo General de las Indias for the History of the Pacific Coast and the American Southwest*. **University of California, Publications in History, vol. 8. Glendale, CA: Arthur H. Clark Co., 1927.**

Although somewhat dated, this guide is still valuable for its documentation of the wealth of records in the General Archives of the Indies dealing with the history of the American Southwest.

**Chávez, Fray Angelico.** *Archives of the Archdiocese of Santa Fe, 1678–1900*. **Publications of the Academy of the American Franciscan History, Bibliographical Series, vol. 3. Washington, DC: Academy of American Franciscan History, 1957.**

This archive is an excellent place to find records about New Mexico.

———. *Origins of New Mexico Families: A Genealogy of the Spanish Colonial Period*. **Santa Fe: Historical Society of New Mexico, 1992.**

Your ancestors may be found in these excellent genealogical studies of early New Mexican families.

**Church of Jesus Christ of Latter-day Saints.** *Resource Papers, Series H. 2. Major Genealogical Record Sources in Mexico.* **Salt Lake City: The Church of Jesus Christ of Latter-day Saints, 1970.**

Reviews the types of records of genealogical interest in Mexico and where they are found.

**Civeira Taboada, Miguel, and Sumano, Maria Elena Bribiesca.** *Archivo General de la Nación: Guía descriptiva de los ramos que constituyen el Archivo General de la Nación.* **Mexico City: Archivo General de la Nación, 1977.**

A detailed guide to the wealth of materials found in the General Archives of the Nation in Mexico City. (Text in Spanish.)

**Colley, Charles C.** *Documents of Southwestern History: A Guide to the Manuscript Collections of the Arizona Historical Society.* **Tucson: Arizona Historical Society, 1972.**

This Society is an excellent place to find records about Hispanic Arizona.

**Colligan, John B.** **"Essential Sources of New Mexico Genealogical Research."** *1992 Buscando Nuestras Raices Seminar, Intermediate and Advanced Strategies.* **Huntington Beach, CA: Society for Hispanic Historic and Ancestral Research, 1992.**

These notes from a seminar on Hispanic genealogy held each year in southern California offer a good review of New Mexican genealogical research.

**Diaz, Albert J.** *A Guide to the Microfilm of Papers Relating to New Mexico Land Grants.* **University of New Mexico Publications, Library Series, No. 1. Albuquerque: University of New Mexico Press, 1960.**

Records of land grants given by the Spanish crown and Mexican government are valuable sources about the families of colonial New Mexico.

*Documentos Relativos a la Independencia de Norteamerica Existentes en Archivos Españoles.* Madrid: Ministerio de Asuntos Exteriores, 1977.

These documents show the important roles that Spaniards played in the American Revolution. (Text in Spanish.)

*English Translation of the Index to El Archivo de Hildalgo del Parral, 1631–1821.* Translated by Consuelo P. Boyd. Tucson: Arizona Silhouettes, 1971.

This is an index to an important colonial municipal archives in northwestern Mexico.

Ericson, Carolyn R. *Nacogdoches—Gateways to Texas: A Biographical Directory, 1773–1849.* Fort Worth, TX: Arrow-Curtis Printing Co., 1974.

Use this resource to find biographies of people in this important Texas town.

Garza, Beatriz Arteaga, and Villaseñor Espinosa, Roberto. *Ramo Californias, 1 y 2; Guías y Catálogos, 3.* Mexico City: Archivo General de la Nación, 1977.

A guide to documents in the Baja and Alta California section of the General Archives of the Nation in Mexico City. (Text in Spanish.)

Gómez Canedo, Lino. *Los archivos de la historia de América, período colonial español.* 2 vols. Instituto Panamericano de Geografía e Historia, Comisión de Historia. Publicación Num. 225. Mexico City: Comisión de Historia, 1961.

A review of collections in many archives worldwide dealing with Spanish colonial history. (Text in Spanish.)

Greenleaf, Richard E., and Meyer, Michael C. *Re-

*search in Mexican Hispanic Topics, Methodology, Sources, and a Practical Guide to Field Research.* Lincoln: University of Nebraska Press, 1973.

One of the best guides for Mexican and borderlands research.

Guerra, Raul J. "How to Use and Understand Diocesan Marriage Investigations and Records of Colonial Mexico." *1992 Buscando Nuestras Raices Seminar: Intermediate and Advanced Strategies.* Huntington Beach, CA: Society for Hispanic Historic and Ancestral Research, 1992.

These notes from a seminar on Hispanic genealogy offer a good introduction to marriage dispensation records, which often include three or four generations of genealogy.

———; Vasquez, Nadine M.; and Vela, Jr. Baldomero. *Index to the Marriage Investigations of the Diocese of Guadalajara, Provinces of Coahuila, Nuevo Leon, Nuevo Santander, Texas, 1653–1750.* Edinburg, TX: University of Texas at Pan American, 1989.

If you have ancestors in colonial Texas, Coahuila, Tamaulipas, or Nuevo Leon, look here to see if they applied for a marriage dispensation.

*Guía de Fuentes para la Historia de Ibero-América Conservados en España.* Madrid: Dirección General de Archivos y Bibliotecas, 1966.

A review of collections in many archives in Spain dealing with Spanish colonial history. (Text in Spanish.)

*Guide to Spanish and Mexican Land Grants in South Texas.* Austin: Texas General Land Office, 1988.

This is a guide to Spanish and Mexican land records in southern Texas. Consult this source if your ancestors owned land in southern Texas.

**Herrera Huerta, Juan Manuel, and San Vicente Tello, Victoria.** *Archivo General de la Nación (México): Guía General.* **Mexico City: Secretaría de Gobernación, 1990.**

A detailed guide to the wonders of the Archivo General de la Nación, complete with multiple illustrations and tips for finding materials in this world-class archive. (Text in Spanish.)

*Indice del Ramo de Provincias Internas, Tomas 1 y 2.* **Mexico City: Archivo General de la Nación, 1967–1974.**

This is a guide to government records dealing with northern Mexico during the late colonial period. (Text in Spanish.)

**Jenkins, Myra E.** *Calendar of the Mexican Archives of New Mexico, 1821–46.* **Santa Fe: State of New Mexico Records Center, 1967.**

————. *Guide to the Microfilms Edition of the Spanish Archives of New Mexico, 1621–1821, in the Archives Division of the State of New Mexico Records Center.* **Santa Fe: State of New Mexico Records Center, 1967.**

The reference works by this author are designed to assist the researcher in accessing these very important New Mexican record collections.

**Kielman, Chester V.** *Guide to the Microfilm Edition of the Bexar Archives, 1717–1803.* **Austin: University of Texas Archives, 1967.**

————. *Guide to the Microfilm Edition of the Bexar Archives, 1804–1821.* **Austin: University of Texas Archives, 1969.**

————. *Guide to the Microfilm Edition of the Bexar Archives, 1822–1836.* **Austin: University of Texas Archives, 1971.**

These reference works assist researchers in accessing these very important Texan record collections.

**Lohmann Villena, Guillermo.** *Los americanos en las órdenes militares.* **Madrid: Consejo Superior de Investigaciones Científicas, 1947.**

There were many colonial Mexicans among the nobles in the honorary societies described in this book. (Text in Spanish.)

**Los Californianos.** *Antepasados* **and** *Noticias para Los Californianos.*

These periodicals published in California by the genealogical association Los Californianos often contain transcriptions and extracts of original records. Check to see whether they are received by the history or genealogy department of your local library, especially if you live in California. (Text in Spanish.)

**Magdaleno, Ricardo.** *Catálogo XX del Archivo General de Simancas, Títulos de Indias.* **Valladolid, Spain: Patronato Nacional de Archivos Historicos, 1954.**

Political appointments and honors granted by the Spanish crown to residents of the European colonies, including New Spain, are indexed in this volume. (Text in Spanish.)

**Naylor, Thomas H., and Polzer, Charles W.** *Northern New Spain. A Research Guide.* **Tucson: University of Arizona Press, 1981.**

This is an excellent introduction to politics and life in northern Mexico and the southwestern United States during the colonial period, as well as to the indexing done by the Documentary Relations of the Southwest Program at the University of Arizona in Tucson.

***New Mexico Genealogist.*** **Albuquerque: New Mexico Genealogical Society, 1962–present.**

For over three decades, the pages of this periodical have contained detailed entries about Hispanics in New Mexico and southern Colorado.

*Newspapers in Microform: Foreign Countries.* **Washington, DC: Library of Congress, 1972–1992.**

Learn which newspapers from Mexico have been microfilmed and are available through interlibrary loan.

**Platt, Lyman D.** *A Genealogical Historical Guide to Latin America.* **Detroit: Gale Research Co., 1978.**

These are guides in English and Spanish about genealogical research in Latin America.

**———.** *México, Guía de Investigaciones Genealógicas.* **Salt Lake City: Instituto Genealógico e Histórico Latinoamericano, 1989.**

This is a general guide to records and research in Mexico. (Text in Spanish.)

**———. "Spanish and Mexican Immigration to the United States."** *Genealogical Journal* **3 (1974): 23–24.**

This is a brief discussion for genealogists of immigration patterns from Mexico to the United States.

**———.** *Una guía genealógico-histórico de latinoamérica.* **Salt Lake City: Acoma, 1977.**

(Text in Spanish.)

**Ryskamp, George R.** *Spanish Military Records.* **Riverside, CA: Hispanic Family History Research, 1987.**

This pamphlet describes how to find and understand military records about your ancestors.

*The Spanish American Genealogist.* **Torrance, CA: The Augustan Society, Inc.**

This periodical, though no longer published, often contained materials on Mexico and the southwestern United States.

**Temple, Thomas Workman II. "Sources for Tracing Spanish-American Pedigrees in the Southwestern United States, Part II: California and Arizona."** *World Conference on Records and Genealogical Seminar, Area F-14b.* **Salt Lake City: The Genealogical Society of the Church of Jesus Christ of Latter-day Saints, 1969.**

Although somewhat dated, this is still a helpful guide to tracing Mexican American ancestry in Arizona and California.

**Tyler, Daniel.** *Sources for New Mexican History 1821–1848.* **Santa Fe: Museum of New Mexico Press, 1984.**

This study is an excellent way to review historical sources available for New Mexico during the Mexican period.

**Woods, Robert D., S. M.** *Index to the Laredo Archives.* **San Antonio: Robert D. Woods, S. M., 1993.**

This is an index to the municipal archives at Laredo, Texas.

**————.** *Reference Materials on Mexican Americans: An Annotated Bibliography.* **Metuchen, NJ: Scarecrow Press, 1976.**

This is a reference work used to access materials about Mexican Americans in several academic disciplines, including guides to genealogical material.

# Chapter 8
# Putting It All Together

When you have reached a good stopping point in your family history research, you will probably want to put your work into a form that can be read and enjoyed by your family members. After all, you deserve to show off a little after all of the hard work you have done.

Some genealogists, after compiling their family data, publish a history of their family in book form. Subsidy publishers, or vanity presses, will publish manuscripts for a fee. Publishing a family history is an impressive achievement, but it is also an expensive and time-consuming undertaking. For now, focus on using the resources at your disposal to make your family history as polished and complete as possible. All you really need is a typewriter or word processor and a lot of creativity to make this happen.

Some family historians write up their family history as a narrative, starting at some point in history and recounting the story of the family up to the present. You might choose to tell the story of your family in reverse chronological order. Or, your family history might be a series of biographical sketches of family members.

Remember that it is crucial to document your sources very carefully when doing your research so that you can cite them when writing your family history. The "facts" of your family history need to be supported with documentation in order to be considered accurate. This way, if you write that your deceased great uncle, Roberto, won a Purple Heart in the Korean war, and your cousin Maria remembers that he won a Medal of Honor, you can show how you obtained your facts using military records. Use footnotes or parenthetical notes to indicate the sources of your information.

Be sure to include a personal history of yourself as part of your family history. Future generations will certainly want to know about you, just as you have been curious about your relatives and ancestors. Write about where and when you were born; schools you have attended; trips you have taken; your interests and goals for the future. Describe jobs you have held, pets you have raised, your favorite friends and teachers. Do you enjoy cooking Mexican foods? Are you an avid reader of Mexican American literature? Do you hope to travel or study in Mexico? Mention these interests as you demonstrate your connection with your Mexican American heritage.

You can make your family history come alive by illustrating it with anything that you feel is meaningful to your family's past: photos, documents, charts, and even recipes, poems, or song lyrics. A copy of your great-grandfather's naturalization record, for example, is not only an informative illustration, but also a tribute to your family's immigrant ancestor. Of course, you will also want to include copies of your completed pedigree charts and family group sheets.

Don't forget to write a foreword to your family history, thanking the family members and other individuals who helped you in your research. You might describe why you decided to trace your roots, mentioning any interesting stories that happened to you along the way. If you like, you can dedicate your family history to a family member who has had a strong influence on your life.

A video family history is another exciting option if you have access to video equipment. Your videotaped oral history interviews can be combined with still shots of maps, photos, heirlooms, or anything else of special meaning to your family. Intersperse your relatives' voices with your own as you explain the important events of your family history.

# Resources

## WRITING YOUR FAMILY HISTORY

**Banks, Keith E.** *How to Write Your Personal and Family History: A Resource Manual.* **Bowie, MD: Heritage Books, 1988.**

This book has much useful information to help you record your family history.

**Barnes, Donald R., and Lackey, Richard S.** *Write It Right: A Manual for Writing Family Histories and Genealogies.* **Ocala, FL: Lyon Press, 1983.**

This book, considered a classic by some genealogists, should be by your side as you undertake to write your family history.

**Fletcher, William P.** *Recording Your Family History.* **New York: Dodd, Mead and Co., 1983.**

A guide to capturing ancestors' memories on tape, audio or video. These tapes can be incorporated into your final family history.

**Glantz, Margo.** *The Family Tree.* **London: Serpent's Tail, 1991.**

A humorous and insightful memoir that traces the history of a Jewish family from its forced emigration from the Ukraine to life in post-revolutionary Mexico. In her exploration of her ancestry and heritage, Glantz, who was born in Mexico, relates the experience of belonging to two distinct cultural traditions and of forging her identity at their interface. This text is an important representation of the Jewish experience in Mexico.

**Gouldrup, Lawrence P.** *Writing the Family Narrative.* **Salt Lake City: Ancestry, Inc., 1987.**

This book is designed for the genealogist who has completed years of research and now wants to put it in book form.

**Kanin, Ruth.** *Write the Story of Your Life.* **Baltimore: Clearfield Co., 1993.**

Try Kanin's suggested exercises for sparking memories and beginning to put your life story in writing.

**Lackey, Richard.** *Cite Your Sources: A Manual for Documenting Family Histories and Genealogical Records.* **New Orleans: Polyanthos, 1980.**

In order to insure accuracy in your work, it is vital that you properly document your sources. This will make it easier for you or other researchers to continue your research. It will also add legitimacy to your project.

**Shull, Wilma Sadler.** *Photographing Your Heritage.* **Salt Lake City: Ancestry, Inc., 1989.**

Shull provides advice on taking photos that will prove valuable when it comes time to illustrate your family history.

**Sturm, Duane, and Sturm, Pat.** *Video Family History.* **Salt Lake City: Ancestry, Inc., 1989.**

A beginner's guide to directing and producing a video family history with a single video camera. Includes suggestions on equipment and techniques such as editing and dubbing.

# Glossary

**alien**  A person living in a country who is not a citizen of that country.

**Alta California**  The name used to differentiate the present state of California from Baja California. The region was a province of Spain and Mexico from 1772 to 1848.

**archives**  A storehouse for original records.

**Baja California**  A peninsula in northwest Mexico between the Pacific Ocean and the Gulf of California, divided into the states of Baja California and Baja California Sur.

*barrio*  Mexican American community in an urban area.

*californio*  Mexican settler in California.

**census record**  A record generated by a government count of a population.

**Church of Jesus Christ of Latter-day Saints (Mormons)**  A religious body that traces its origin to Joseph Smith in 1830 and accepts the Book of Mormon as divine revelation. Genealogy is an endeavor of religious significance to the Mormons because of their belief that ancestors who have been identified by genealogical research are considered to be baptized as Mormons when a descendant is Mormon.

**civil register**  In Mexico, a government repository for documents such as birth, marriage, and death records.

*colonia*  Community formed by Mexican immigrants near the farms where they worked.

**locality analysis**  The step of determining an ancestor's point of departure and seeking information about the location.

*luminaria*  Christmas lantern made of a candle set in a paper bag.

**memorabilia**   Items that provide information about the past.

*mestizaje*   The process of becoming mestizo; the mixing of races.

**mestizo**   Person of mixed races, such as Indian and Spanish.

*municipio*   City or municipality.

*mutualista*   Mexican American mutual aid society.

**notarial record**   A document authorized by a public officer recording information about an event, such as a wedding.

*nuevomexicano*   Spanish-speaking settler in New Mexico.

*pachucos*   Young Mexican American men who wore zoot suits in the 1940s.

**parish record**   Record kept by a church about members.

**pedigree chart**   A chart that allows for the recording of information about one's ancestors.

*posada*   Religious procession with statues of saints; householders along the route are expected to provide food and shelter.

**preliminary survey**   The recommended first four steps of a genealogical search: collecting family documents, asking questions of family members, visiting a LDS Family History Center, and checking the library for any published family histories.

**siblings**   Brothers and sisters.

**surname**   Last name, or family name.

**tamales**   Dish of minced meat and cornmeal wrapped in corn husks.

*tejano*   Mexican settler in Texas.

**vital record**   A government or church document that records a major life event, such as a birth, marriage, or death.

**zoot suit**   A distinctive style of dress adopted by some Mexican American teenage boys in the 1940s, consisting of a long coat, baggy pants that fit tightly at the ankles, and a broad-brimmed hat.

# Index

## ABOUT THE AUTHORS

**George R. Ryskamp** has researched Hispanic family history for twenty-five years. A member of the Association of Professional Genealogists, he is also the author of *Tracing Your Hispanic Heritage* and *Finding Your Hispanic Roots*. **Peggy Ryskamp** has researched Hispanic family history with her husband for the past fifteen years. They live in Orem, Utah, with their four children.

## ILLUSTRATION CREDITS

Cover, © Alan Becker/The Image Bank; cover inset and pp. viii, 3, 20, 24, 26, 28, 32, 34, 68, 70, 74, 83, 85, 86, 87, 145, BETTMANN; p. 15, © Will McIntyre/Mexican Government Tourism Office; p. 114, courtesy of the Mexican Government Tourism Office. *Color insert:* pp. 2, 4, 7, © J. J. Foxx/NYC; pp. 3, 10, 11, 14, 15, BETTMANN; p. 5, © Tatiana Parcero/Mexican Government Tourism Office; p. 6, courtesy of the Mexican Government Tourism Office; pp. 8, 9, © Jack Kurtz/Impact Visuals; p. 12, © Donna DeCesare/Impact Visuals; p. 13, courtesy of Repertorio Español; p.16, © Michael Salas/The Image Bank.

## LAYOUT AND DESIGN

Kim Sonsky